FAMILIA

ULSTER GENEALOGICAL REVIEW

Ulster
Genealogical
& Historical
Guild

I0094142

NUMBER 11
1995

incorporating Ulster Genealogical & Historical Guild *Newsletter*

Copyright 1995
Reprinted 2007

Published by
Ulster Historical Foundation
12 College Square East
Belfast
BT1 6DD

ISBN 0-901905-73-9

Cover design by Dunbar Design
Printed by ColourBooks Ltd, Dublin

Front cover illustration: Famine scene from
Illustrated London News
Back cover illustration: Early Seventeenth Century map of Ulster

CONTENTS

EDITORIAL

Familia first appeared in December 1985 and this edition marks the tenth anniversary of a publication which aims to provide informed writing on sources and case studies relating to that area where history and genealogy overlap with mutual benefit. This volume is not the first, nor will it be the last, to look at the 150th anniversary of the onset of the Famine in 1845. And although there is a strong case to be made for a more suitable commemoration of this pivotal event in Irish history in, say, 1996 and particularly 1997, since it was the successive failures of the potato crop which extended the scale of want and disease to uncontrollable proportions, it was considered appropriate to include this topic in *Familia's* agenda.

Several of the articles and reviews consider important characteristics of migration from Ireland which developed as a consequence of the Great Famine. Brenda Collins analyses the acceleration in the removals of Irish people to Great Britain and, in doing so, reminds us that emigration, far from having its roots solely in the Famine, had in fact been gathering pace in the previous 30 years, to North America and Australia as well as to Britain. Ian McKeane continues this theme by outlining the steps taken recently in Liverpool, in the shape of a major centre for famine migration, to acknowledge the travails and travels of famine refugees. John McGuckin's description of his family's migration from north Antrim to Pennsylvania in the post-famine era reminds us of the continuing implications of the Famine throughout the remainder of the nineteenth century. The review of *Oceans of Consolation,* David Fitzpatrick's lyrical analysis of the letters of Irish emigrants to Australia completes the survey of the Irish diaspora in modern times.

George Ruddock's narrative on the life and work of Amy Carmichael in India is a timely reminder of one other significant feature of the Irish abroad – their missionary work – which saw, and continues to see, Irish men and women of all religions serving in many parts of the developing world. The writings of Richard Clarke and J. Fred Rankin are already well known to the discerning genealogist. In this volume Professor Clarke relays the benefit of his role as archivist of the internationally renowned Royal Victoria

Hospital and provides an account of the archive under his control. Fred Rankin's essay on the genealogical background to his wife Kathleen's family is a very informative example of how a family study can be undertaken in which 'inside' knowledge is amplified by a skilful use of generally accessible sources. One of George Chambers's two reviews develops his research, which featured in his article in last year's issue of *Familia*, on the business families of Ulster (particularly Belfast) in the nineteenth century.

My own review of the publication of the Irish Linen Centre, which is located at the award-winning Lisburn Museum, acknowledges the worth of this very fine museum; it is also an appropriate means of marking my own recent translation from the world of archives to the Ulster Museum, where I am Keeper of History.

Trevor Parkhill

CONTRIBUTORS

George Chambers is the Vice-Chairman of the Ulster Historical Foundation.

Richard Clarke is Chairman of the Ulster Historical Foundation and author of over 30 titles in its *Gravestone Inscription* Series.

Brenda Collins is curator of the Irish Linen Centre of Lisburn Museum and a demographic historian.

John H. McGuckin Jr is a member of the Ulster Genealogical and Historical Guild and has previously written in *Familia* on aspects of his family's history.

Ian McKeane lectures in history at the Institute of Irish Studies in the University of Liverpool and is secretary of the city's Great Famine Commemoration Committee.

J. Fred Rankin is a retired businessman and local historian who has written and published extensively on sources for genealogy.

George Ruddock, who lives in Portadown, Co Armagh, has taught in schools in Northern Ireland and India for some 30 years.

Rev. Dr David Stewart's article was first published in 1954 by the Presbyterian Historical Society and is here reproduced in slightly edited form.

Trevor Parkhill is Keeper of History in the Ulster Museum, Belfast and editor of *Familia*.

IRISH EMIGRATION TO BRITAIN DURING THE FAMINE DECADE 1841-51:

by Brenda Collins

Over eight million people emigrated from Ireland during the nineteenth century. Every generation contributed to a greater or lesser degree to this movement which was already entrenched before the Famine. The effects of the Famine years were to bring about an extension of the concept of emigration from one of betterment for the few to one of simple survival for the many. This was equally true in the case of emigration to north America, to Australasia or to Britain. Of course migrants had been moving back and forth across the Irish Sea for centuries and by the mid-eighteenth century there were Irish neighbourhoods described as such in London. It was only in the nineteenth century that the first reliable statistics on these sorts of migrations began to emerge, and it is fortunate for historians of the Famine that these provide evidence of the effects of the Famine upon Irish migration patterns to Great Britain.

The first national census to record the number of Irish people in Great Britain was in 1841 when there were 415,000 Irish-born people recorded as living there. This was in fact 77 per cent of all known Irish-born emigrants world wide and shows the extent to which the flow of migrants to Britain set the pattern for subsequent movement to other parts of the world. Between 1851 and 1881 each successive British census recorded about three quarters of a million Irish-born residents and during the 70 years from 1851 to 1921 the number of Irish-born people living in Britain was always about one quarter of all the Irish migrants throughout the world.

During the Famine decade of 1841-1851 the number of Irish-born people in Great Britain rose to 727,000 – a rise of 40 per cent from the 415,000 of the 1841 census. These figures probably underestimate the number of Irish people arriving in Britain in the 1840s; the real figure may have been nearer 350,000. As the total emigration from Ireland in the Famine decade was at least one million, we can see that the migrant stream to Britain was probably about one third of all the emigrants who left Ireland.

Although emigration was widespread in Ireland it drew on certain sections of society more than others. More emigrants came from the adolescent and young adult age groups than from among older people and much of the emigrant movement consisted of those unencumbered with families. Certainly family emigration did exist during the late 1840s; generally, however, the Irish emigrant to Britain was most likely to be an unmarried adult. This should not imply that he or she travelled alone but reinforces the point that their entry to the British workforce was at the precise time when their labour input was maximised without the burden of dependants.

A second general feature of Irish emigration to Britain throughout the nineteenth century was the virtual parity of the sexes. Certainly, in the general movement to Britain there were migrant harvesters and navvies, close knit male groups often moving from specific origins to particular destinations, and in Scotland there was always a slight majority of Irish men. Nevertheless, women were as equal a proportion of each Irish immigrant generation in Britain as they were elsewhere.

About their religious badges, less can be said with certainty. The sheer volume of settlement means that overall the Catholic Irish were the most numerous, but this is not to say that in specific pockets or neighbourhoods and, at particular points in time, Protestant folk did not predominate. The issue of identity was one of perception; as Catholic characteristics became identified as Irish characteristics whether of lifestyle, diet or cultural behaviour then those Irish people who did not appear to share those characteristics became un-Irish and took the more amorphous identity of the urban working class in Britain.

Regardless of regional differences within Ireland in its pattern and chronology, emigration came, for the individual, to represent an expected option to be considered at a stage in his or her life, and children were reared in that knowledge. Migration in search of fame and fortune, from the country to the city, is a world-wide historical and modern phenomenon. For the Irish, who had only one city with rapid growth in the nineteenth century (Belfast), the 'fame and fortune' ideal had to be concentrated outside the island. As the nearest place that wasn't Ireland, Britain and its towns provided the first

2

and cheapest destination. The three main routes established in the early nineteenth century were Derry and Belfast to Glasgow, Cork to Bristol and London and Dublin to Liverpool. To some extent the regional distribution of Irish people in Great Britain reflected these routes and their catchment areas. Thus Irish settlement in Scotland tended to originate from the northern half of Ireland, while those in southern England tended to have emigrated from Munster and Leinster. Emigrants from Connacht sailed from Dublin to Liverpool and then moved on to the Lancashire and Yorkshire industrial towns.

The Journey
What were the conditions of travel for such emigrants? We can probably all remember the old Heysham and Liverpool boats and it does not take a lot of imagination to identify to some degree with those folk in the mid-nineteenth century who were considerably weaker physically, lacking the money which might have bought them physical comforts and also frightened by authority and by the strangeness of their situation. Steam boat passenger services had begun to operate across the Irish Sea in the 1820s. By the 1840s many operated daily, once or twice weekly according to seasonal demand. (FIG. 1)

Baggage and livestock had first priority on the Liverpool steamers, and the poor Irish huddled without shelter on the open decks, packed shoulder to shoulder, 'holding on to each other, and to anything else they could lay hold onto to keep from being washed overboard: one ship's officer admitted crowding 1400 emigrants onto a single vessel and many passengers had to stand throughout the entire voyage... Even cabin passengers such as Mary Cumming, who awoke in her berth with a dead rat beneath her head, were ecstatic to reach Liverpool.' (Miller, 1985, p.253)

Some voyages had very tragic outcomes. In 1851 an inquest was held at Whitechapel workhouse in London on the body of Mary Collins, aged 45, a poor Irish emigrant brought from the *Duke of Cambridge* which had sailed from Cork. The body of the deceased was in a most emaciated condition and covered with bruises as if she had been severely ill-used. Two of the deceased's children were on board with her.The ship's surgeon 'found her lying upon that

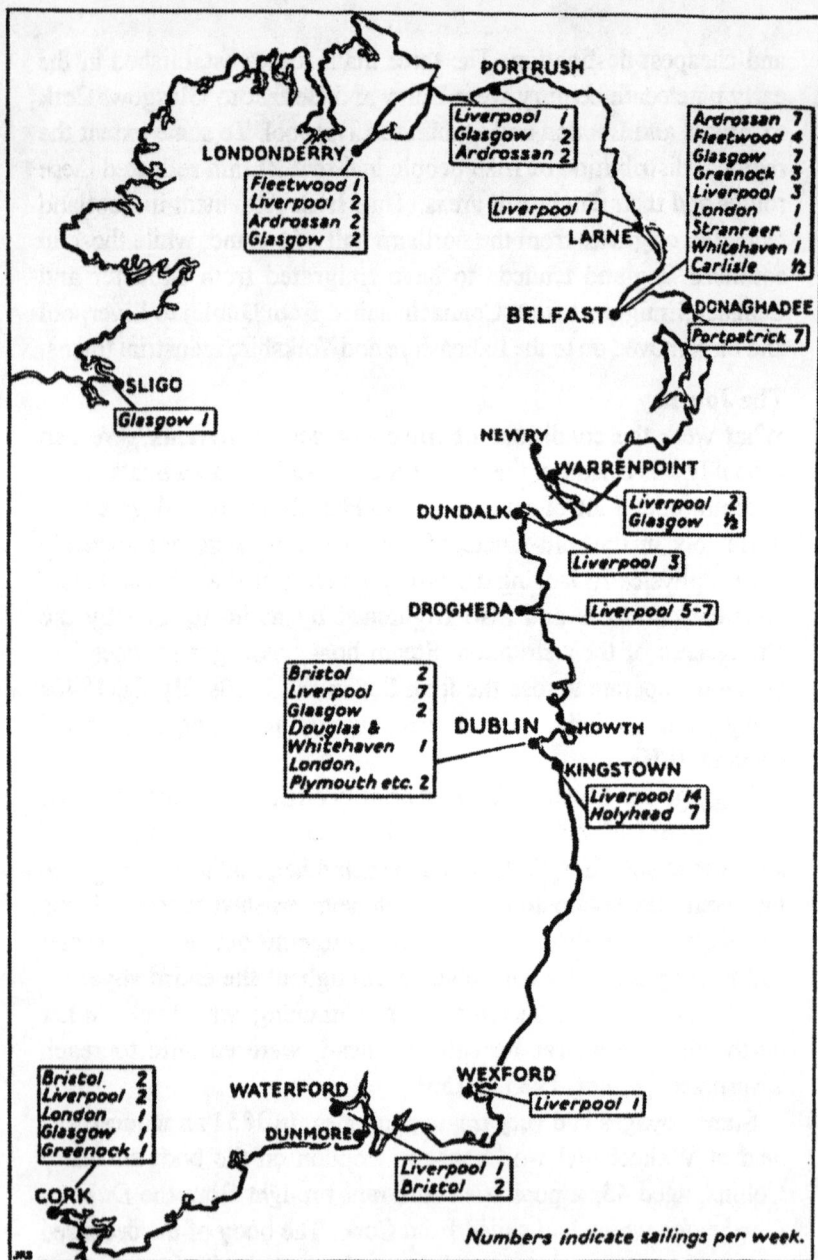

PORTRUSH

Liverpool 1
Glasgow 2
Ardrossan 2

LONDONDERRY

Fleetwood 1
Liverpool 2
Ardrossan 2
Glasgow 2

Ardrossan 7
Fleetwood 4
Glasgow 7
Greenock 3
Liverpool 3
London 1
Stranraer 1
Whitehaven 1
Carlisle ½

Liverpool 1

LARNE

BELFAST

DONAGHADEE

Portpatrick 7

SLIGO

Glasgow 1

NEWRY

WARRENPOINT

DUNDALK

Liverpool 2
Glasgow ½

Liverpool 3

DROGHEDA

Liverpool 5-7

Bristol 2
Liverpool 7
Glasgow 2
Douglas &
Whitehaven 1
London,
Plymouth etc. 2

DUBLIN

HOWTH

KINGSTOWN

Liverpool 14
Holyhead 7

WEXFORD

Bristol 2
Liverpool 2
London 1
Glasgow 1
Greenock 1

WATERFORD

Liverpool 1

DUNMORE

Liverpool 1
Bristol 2

CORK

Numbers indicate sailings per week.

FIG. 1
Map indicating the ports in Ireland from which passengers sailed to
ports in Britain. Also given is the number of sailings per week.

part of the vessel appropriated for the use of cattle. There was nothing under her and all her clothing consisted of a blanket, a ragged gown and a chemise. She was quite pulseless and perfectly speechless.' The captain said 'he had a very boisterous voyage and the emigrants had been exposed to the inclemency of the weather... he had brought over between 400 and 500 and was in the habit of bringing over a similar number every week....Patrick Collins, the son of the deceased, said his mother was discharged from the workhouse in Schull. They walked to Cork, a distance of 50 miles and embarked on the boat. His brother, who was in Greenwich, sent his mother six shillings to pay the expenses of the voyage. Mr Nash, the workhouse superintendent said 'the deceased died from typhus fever, which had no doubt been accelerated by the overcrowding of the vessel and exposure to the weather'. (Davis, 1991, p.44)

As well as the individual tragedies there were also major incidents. The tragic story of the *Londonderry* sailing from Sligo to Liverpool in December 1848 and carrying 177 passengers intending to sail on to America became a classic. On the voyage a storm blew up off the north-west coast of Ireland and the passengers were put below decks and the hatch secured with ropes. Within a confined space of 307 square feet, 174 people struggled for lack of air and water. In the storm, the lights went out, people suffocated and collapsed and were trampled on. Eventually when the hatch was removed, it was discovered that 72 people had died. (Davis, 1991, p.44)

Such happenings were not representative of all the sailings. They were indeed the exceptional ones which made the news. Nevertheless the fact that they happened and the manner of their reporting coloured the reputation both of the emigrant ships and of the people who travelled in them. As the coroner at Mary Collins' inquest commented, 'it was to be regretted that this system of emigration was allowed as it caused so many mendicants to be in this country'.

Employment patterns
It was in agricultural work rather than in the towns that Irish people were first noted in any numbers. Seasonal farm work provided cash for those who came to Britain to earn enough to pay the rent on Irish farms and to buy goods to supplement their marginal existence. The

frugal lifestyle of the migrant harvesters, living in their employers' barns and sheds, and working all the daylight hours, enabled them to maximise their savings. Their thriftiness and mobility also released the farmers from the responsibility of providing for a year-round workforce, either in terms of jobs or housing or rateable support for parish poor relief. The vast majority of Irish seasonal workers were cottiers or small farmers and their kinsmen – the self-selected and able-bodied who were likely to reap the most rewards. Even before the Famine, during the 1841 census, which was taken in June, a tally was reckoned of harvest migrants leaving Irish ports. Of the 57,000 who were counted, most came from Connacht. It has been calculated that the numbers listed from Mayo and Roscommon were the equivalent of one person for every six and eight households respectively in that one summer alone. The number of young men who, during their lifetimes, would have gone at least once to work in Britain was thus very large, as was the number of families who benefited. This pattern of temporary movement persisted through the century and indeed into the present day as a means of keeping the family farm together. What was distinctive about the Famine emigration was that it was permanent, with very little intention or likelihood of return.

Most Irish Famine emigrants to Britain settled in the places which offered the greatest job opportunities, the towns and cities which were being created by the Industrial Revolution. The early pattern persisted; by 1841 just under half of the Irish in Britain lived in four of the biggest cities, London, Liverpool, Manchester and Glasgow. In 1851 after the main Famine rush, the population of Liverpool was 22 per cent Irish, of Glasgow 18 per cent. A comparatively small town, Dundee, had 19 per cent of its population Irish-born, nearly one in five. The largest numbers were of course in London, 109,000 people, though they made up only 4.6 per cent of city's population. Through the rest of the century there was a gradual diffusion of Irish settlement to smaller, rapidly growing towns at the same time as there was increasing drift from the English countryside to the towns. Thus first-generation Irish immigrants settled in to urban life in Britain alongside first-generation rural movers. The one exception to this was seen in the continuing dominant attraction of Glasgow and the Strathclyde region for, in every decade until the First World War, nearly ten per cent of all the Irish people in Britain lived in Glasgow. Irish settlement was a reflection of the fact that urban nineteenth-century Britain was a set of local labour markets. This can be seen most readily in gender-specific occupations. Textile towns in particular afforded mill and factory work to girls and women: Dundee, the linen and jute town, had twice as many young Irish women as men in the mid century. A comment from Hull as early as 1836 confirms the relationship: 'There are few Irish in Hull because we have no large factories to afford them employment'. Similarly in military and naval towns such as Colchester and Plymouth there were more Irish men than women, just as in those towns as a whole. Later in the century the distribution of heavy industry was important. Barrow in Furness grew rapidly after 1860 as a shipbuilding centre in the north-west which attracted Irish men. Other male-dominated clusters of Irish working men were to be found in the coal and ironstone mining areas of Lanark, north-east England and south Wales.

Where specifically local constraints were absent, there was a considerable sameness about the types of jobs which Irish immigrants took up, both at different times and in different towns. This is partly explained by their position as adult migrants, too old to be apprenticed to a trade and lacking skills except stamina and desperation for work. They worked in the docks and warehousing construction in London, Liverpool and other ports. Others became street traders or general shopkeepers dealing in basic provisions, clothing or hardware. Street trading was the refuge of any casual labourer, Irish or not. In Glasgow in the 1830s and 1840s the Irish were said to have 'all the elements of the mercantile character, they are very fond of bargain making, of buying and selling and of adventure'.

If the most common Irish man's job was as a labourer, the most typical Irish woman's work was in service, as domestic servants, charwomen and laundresses. The administrative and commercial towns were most likely to support families with servants – at mid-century almost one quarter of the Irish working women in York and Liverpool and over half of those in Bristol were in service. Personal networks and chain migration played a large part in retaining initial patterns of Irish settlement. Irish workers in the Greenock sugar refineries were introduced by friends and relatives already in employment. Mill owners sent to Ireland to supplement their workforce when they needed extra hands. Indeed, Irish family patterns did to some extent define the pace of industrial expansion. Cotton, linen, wool and silk towns had a mainly adolescent workforce – 'without the Irish', a Manchester cotton mill owner said, 'there would have been a want of children for the factory employments', – but children came with their parents and many of their fathers were hand loom weavers, continuing in industries which were already undermined by mechanisation. They carried on with their trades and to some extent their presence delayed the adoption of technological innovation particularly in the mid-century Dundee linen industry and the Lancashire cotton industry.

Residential Patterns

The networks which created their occupational profile also gave rise to identifiable Irish quarters or streets in numerous towns or cities as well as dispersal among the general inhabitants. The Irish districts in Victorian towns fell into two main types. Firstly there were the older, previously grand houses which had been subdivided to house eight or ten families. Dickens described the tall rookeries of St Giles in London, which had infill of cottages creating masses of dense housing with no direct street access. These were dead end locations, literally and figuratively. Manchester, York and Glasgow had many examples of these where Irish people and other poor wretches lived. Living quarters were mixed up with stables, cowsheds and the apparatus of small scale food and animal processing and dealing in poultry, fish, offal and rags. For some social commentators in the 1840s, 1850s and 1860s places such as 'Little Ireland' in Manchester with its 'black smoke, polluted rivers, unpaved streets, smell of pig sties, privies and open sewers coupled with the filthy cramped dwellings with their barren damp interiors' were directly associated with the hordes of Irish immigrants.

More degrading still were the cellar dwellings of cities such as Liverpool and also Glasgow and Edinburgh, which, being below ground, were liable to flood from foul and fresh water. Many of the

Famine emigrants in Liverpool found themselves living in such conditions, sometimes with several families to a room. The reality of this existence was often a far cry from the expectations of the emigrants, fostered by hearsay of easy jobs and good money and by the land agents, clergy and authorities in Ireland who saw emigration as a panacea for the troubled country. (FIG. 2)

A second pattern of Irish residence was in newer town housing built not in the town centres but on the outskirts, and initially therefore outside civic jurisdiction. This was quickly erected to minimal standards for fast profits to cater for the masses of rural immigrants, Irish and others. Back to back houses with no rear access were typical of such buildings lived in by the Irish in Leeds and Cardiff. Obviously residential choices were determined by rent levels. At mid-century, rents for a two or three roomed newly built cottage were typically four or five shillings, compared with a labourer's average earnings of 12 shillings per week. Hence rooms were sublet and bed space was shared, leading to the succinct observation that the homes of the Irish contained more people than furniture. This was viewed as an inevitable consequence of industrial growth for as one Dundee town councillor explained in the 1840s, 'in a town like Dundee, where trade fluctuates so much, we of course have a rush of people into it and of course a number of families go into one house and live in it'.

Ultimately all the studies of first generation Irish communities in Britain have found that they were more likely to have lodgers and more of them, than other town dwellers even those in similar circumstances. Such actions minimised outlay on rent and reinforced ties with other Irish immigrants. For the young without family ties, lodgings were the only accommodation outside the workhouse and in many cases there was a distant family or birthplace link arising from chain migration. This was a response to the hurried in-movement of the late 1840s. The second and third generations were less likely to follow this pattern, as has been documented for Lancashire in the 1870s, though taking in lodgers was still the resort of those in casual work when money was tight, and particularly by Irish widows in troubled circumstances.

In many towns, certain districts became identified as 'Irish', an attribution which persisted sometimes well into this century until slum clearance took place. Within these districts, however, there could be a rapid turnover of population as Irish families moved about, like any others, taking advantage of cheaper rents, or greater charity, or just anticipating eviction. Neighbourhood contacts especially of shopping and credit networks were important and encouraged Irish people to stick with what they knew. Another factor leading to the consolidated image of Irish districts was the practical need to live within the sound of the mill bell as in Leeds and Dundee, near the docks in Liverpool or near the clothing warehouses and sweatshops in London. Urban living for the Irish was circumscribed by locally available jobs, limited mobility and dependence on the familiar – 'all that lay beyond a tiny circle of personal acquaintances or walking distance was darkness'. Irish families were attached to their neighbourhoods – 'they feel almost as if they were coming to an Irish town and though they have little to give, they give what they have'.

In the immediate aftermath of the Famine immigration, another feature which English commentators saw as characteristic of Irish districts, and therefore of Irish people, was a high level of disease and ill-health. Overcrowding, lodgers, dependence on casual earnings and the trauma of uprooting provided conditions where infectious diseases could spread rapidly with devastating effects in a period when the basic causes of diseases such as typhus and cholera were not fully understood even by medical men. Many Irish people journeyed to Britain only to succumb to infection and die in a workhouse in Liverpool or London. Part of the fear expressed in the prejudices of English officialdom whether in charge of the emigrants' shipping, housing or poor relief, was related to the perception of the immigrant Irish as the spreaders of killer diseases and epidemics. Public health officials as far apart as Cardiff and Bradford identified the Irish invasions in their towns as the main causes of disease in the late 1840s. 'We are accustomed to associate notions of filth, squalor and beggarly destitution with everything Irish, from the large number of lazy, idle and wretched natives of the Sister Isle who are continually crossing our paths.' (Davis, 1991, p.65)

FIG. 2

HEIGHT OF IMPUDENCE.

Irishman to John Bull. — "Spare a thrifle, yer Honour, for a poor Irish Lad to buy a bit of — a Blunderbuss with."

FIG. 3

Catholicism and Anti-Irishness

For many Irish immigrants membership of the Catholic church was a badge of cultural identity. However, it is also important to realise how much the Catholic church in England was altered by the Irish influx of the post-Famine period. Cardinal Manning reminisced in the 1880s that he had spent his life 'working for the Irish occupation of England'. Probably by the early twentieth century between half and three-quarters of all Catholics in England were Irish by birth or descent. Similarly, within the framework of the British Isles as a whole, nearly one third of all Roman Catholics lived not in Ireland but in the urban dioceses of England and Wales.

During the 1850s there were not enough clergy and this shortage was compounded by language and dialect difficulties. In south Wales in the 1850s an Italian parish priest compiled a conversation book in Irish so that he could hear confessions. Until more Catholic churches were built, missions among the urban poor were successful, especially among Irish women and children who saw the 'fayther' as their point of reference in dealing with the wider community. A much larger number who did not attend the missions nevertheless retained or maybe adopted a Catholic identity which was increasingly equated, by others, with Irish patriotism; a London Irish street sweeper described himself to Henry Mayhew in the 1860s as 'being a Catholic for I'm not ashamed to own my religion before any man' while his Cockney-born workmate with lukewarm religious convictions and non-attendance at church saw the Catholic church as offering 'an Irish religion [that he] wasn't to be expected to understand'.

In both England and Scotland the Irish presence aroused much anti-Catholicism which mixed theological and moral objections. The Scots' antagonism had two additional elements, the first of which was the relatively high proportion of Irish Protestants in its Irish immigrant population. Over the whole nineteenth century in Scotland, between one quarter and one third of the new arrivals from Ireland were Presbyterians, Episcopalians and Methodists. These immigrants brought with them a cultural baggage of social distinctions which was already neatly labelled. Secondly, anti-Catholicism was an ideology which had bound together all urban Lowlanders since the mid-eighteenth century. Such feelings were fuelled by colourful preachers who travelled through Britain and agitated and titillated their audiences with a mixture of drama and diatribe against Catholic religious practice.

The response of the Irish communities to anti-Catholicism was often one of retrenchment. The mid century religious missions sought to capture and retain their flocks by parish-based clubs and the inculcation of the habit of regular financial contributions. From this developed the duplication and reproduction at local parish level of many of the non-Catholic and secular social institutions of the Victorian era. The development of the Catholic school system in England was one example of this. The Church tried consciously to dominate the whole non-working lives of its members and their families. In return, Church membership offered the immigrant an accepted place in an otherwise alien situation and also practical aid in the form of friendly society, sick and burial schemes and eventually loans for house purchase. Membership of local confraternities also gave a fellowship of associations beyond the immediate locality in bodies such as St Vincent de Paul. Such membership offered most Irish men the main opportunity to display their distance from the rough counter cultures of drink and petty crime which were considered part of the neighbourhoods of the 'low Irish'.

The charges of criminality and threats to public order made against the Irish were usually attributable to drink rather than to innate evil. The Irish were certainly arrested more frequently than the English or Scots and their pattern of listed offences tended to be offences against the person, assault and breaches of the peace rather than offences against property. Drunkenness on a Saturday night combined with noisy and casual violence invited attention to Irish neighbourhoods and reinforced popular perceptions of the need to control the Irish.

Another of the British responses to the threat of social disorder was seen in the interpretation of elegibility for poor relief of Irish Famine immigrants. Because there was no welfare state or central organisation of welfare, local attitudes determined the method as well as the degree of help. During the Famine many Irish applicants swarmed into workhouses in the north-west and north of England. Elsewhere they were excluded from local authority responsibility and were directed to alternative charitable or church-based agencies on the grounds of being Irish and Catholic. In Scotland, the parish residence qualifications were raised from three to five years. Many Scottish and some English parishes deported Irish people back to Ireland in the late 1840s and 1850s. The cholera epidemic during 1849 spread to Ireland from Britain, through a deported immigrant returning to Belfast from Liverpool. Fear of removal caused many Irish Famine immigrant folk to turn to their own networks for survival and may have discouraged their children and grandchildren from identification with the rights and duties of citizenship in late Victorian Britain.

The view of the Irish as harbingers of disease, as parasites on the rates, as cheap labour and strikebreakers, and as threats to the social order combined in political invective and cartoons which neatly discouraged overt sympathy with the immigrants' plight. (FIG.3) The possibility that Ireland and Irish people would bite the hand that fed them was a commonly expressed fear. After the middle of the century this was also overlaid with notions of racial superiority which were to be given intellectual reinforcement by Darwin's theories on evolution. In the forms of the political cartoonists, the Irish man was given ape-like features implying he was of a different social order of being to the John Bulls of England.

Irish emigration did not end when the Famine conditions in Ireland lessened. As with Irish emigration patterns to other countries, in some ways this was only the beginning. For each subsequent generation born in Ireland there has been a proportion who have left to settle in Britain, joining the descendants of earlier Irish settlers. The question of 'Irishness' then becomes at the one time diluted by descent and sometimes strengthened by allegiance. The Irish communities include all those of Irish birth and those who have chosen to claim Irish descent as well as those who may have had that claim thrust upon them. The balance of these groups has shifted though perception has not always found it expedient to acknowledge this. Many have become absorbed into the general lifestyles of urban working-class Britain and have sought their methods of advancement through them. Currently Irish studies is an immensely popular subject in Britain at all levels of education. The opportunity to study the

Famine and all its effects without recriminations or blame seems such a rich one, at this moment in political time, that we cannot afford to pass it by.

FURTHER READING

Poor Enquiry, Ireland. Appendix G, State of the Irish Poor in Great Britain. P.P. 1836 XXXIV.

Brenda Collins 'The Irish in Britain 1780-1921' in B.J. Graham and L.J. Proudfoot eds. *An Historical Geography of Ireland.* (Academic Press, London, 1993)

Graham Davis *The Irish in Britain 1815-1914.* (Gill & MacMillan, Dublin, 1991)

Kerby Miller *Emigrants and Exiles.* (Oxford University Press, Oxford, 1985)

COMMEMORATING OUR FAMINE FOREBEARS

by Ian McKeane

The linkage of the UHF *Famine Forebears* genealogy conference with the *Hungry Stream* Conference at the Ulster-American Folk Park, Omagh, Co. Tyrone in early September provided the opportunity to hear and meet an array of expert speakers who gave insights into various facets of the calamity of *An Gorta Mhor*, the Great Hunger. The *Hungry Stream* was my reason for going back to Ulster although the opportunity to further my own genealogical research and perhaps to do a bit of fishing helped to justify the trip.

As a direct descendant of a professional soldier born in Armagh city in 1812 who married a farmer's daughter from west Tyrone in 1848 and came to Britain in 1853, I have been struck by the coincidence of the dates of the Famine (1847-52) and of my ancestor's marriage and eventual settling in Britain. My great grandparents were not driven directly by hunger but, on leaving the Inniskilling Dragoons, opportunity was to be found in Britain and not in Tyrone. The rural economy there had collapsed and there were few openings for an ex-cavalry sergeant and his young family. Their wanderings are traced by the birthplaces of my great uncles, Dublin and Dundalk, and of my grandfather born in York in England. They finally settled in Lanark, Scotland. Why exactly they ended up there is not clear but the situation in Tyrone did play a considerable part in their emigration.

In many accounts of the Famine which followed the blight on the potato crop between the years 1845-52, the effects on the population of the nine counties of Ulster tend to be eclipsed by the devastation caused in Munster and Connacht. The visual images which come down to us are James Mahoney's prints of the ragged dispossessed of west Cork desperately attempting to survive. (One was used on this year's UHF's conference publicity leaflet). Similarly, the increase in emigration of those with enough strength and means to do so was fuelled in large measure by people from the other three provinces of Ireland. Yet, the province of Ulster was profoundly affected by the Famine. Patterns of hardship elsewhere in Ireland were replicated in Ulster. It was the rural poor west of the Bann who suffered most.

More substantial farmers suffered from the collapse of the rural economy and landlords and agents displayed a similar variety of response as they did elsewhere in Ireland. While some like the Drapers' Company in Co. Londonderry did their best to alleviate the suffering, others seized the opportunity to evict tenants to consolidate holdings or, as at Castle Ward in Co. Down, to improve the view. At the same time the textile industry in Ulster was evolving which meant that the cottage weavers were finding it increasingly difficult to compete with the mills of Belfast and the growing towns of the Lagan valley. As rents were not paid and the towns attracted the starving in search of work or charity, a sense of catastrophe became widespread. Fairs and markets registered a downturn in goods bought and sold. Violence and the threat of civil disorder were reported in Newry, Co. Armagh, south Donegal and Inishowen as the decade came to a close. At best a re-dimensioning of the economy was taking place, at worst the rural economy temporarily collapsed.

This was the atmosphere at the time my great grandparents married and then took the decision to leave Ulster. The young Tyrone girl followed her soldier, leaving her parent's grave in Ardstraw for ever – a grave topped by a stone with space enough for the names of a dozen descendants. Like in so many Ulster families, descendants there were to be, but they lie buried across the sea.

The Ordnance Survey memoirs of the 1830s paint a picture of pre-famine Tyrone with small towns and a countryside divided between richer lowland holdings largely in Protestant hands and the higher, rougher holdings in Catholic hands. Irish was still widely spoken by the latter. Crops were oats, barley, flax and potatoes. Emigration is noted as being slight in the parishes where any reference is made to it. The first attack of blight in 1845 in Tyrone was not too severe since many of the tubers were sound despite the attack on the tops. An excellent oat harvest mitigated the effects to some extent. But by the following winter things were much worse. February 1847 was bitter with heavy snow and a correspondent described what he saw near Omagh in a letter to the Board of Works: 'the weaker and worse clad, and perhaps badly fed, workmen were not able to endure it' (J. Bardon, *A History of Ulster*, p 289).

Although the mortality rate in Tyrone was lower than that in neighbouring Co. Armagh the population loss in the period nearly matched the average for the whole of Ireland. In 1841 the total rural population was 298,500 but by 1851 it had decreased to around 241,000, a drop of 19%. Overall, the nine counties of Ulster provided some 40% of the total emigration from Ireland in the years 1847-8.

The ports of Sligo, Derry, Belfast, Newry and Dundalk provided passages to North America, principally to Canada and Boston either direct or via Glasgow or Liverpool. Liverpool provided the double attraction of a greater range of cheap passages and being itself the gateway to the English industrial regions. Consequently, much of the 'Hungry Stream' flooded into the Clarence Dock in Liverpool and, although much of the flood then continued its flow across the Atlantic, significant eddies remained. Despite the difficulties that England's industries were going through in the late 1840s the industrial towns of the north of England, many within a few days walk from Liverpool, were seen as areas of possible salvation. Many emigrants lost what resources they had to those Liverpool street-sharks who preyed on them. This condemned them to obtain shelter in the courts and cellars of the poorest areas of the city and seek relief locally. The city population increased suddenly and dramatically by 31% in the 1840s. Overcrowding and resultant disease led to an appalling death rate in Liverpool during the Famine years. But many migrants survived and, as even a quick look at the telephone book will show, their descendants now form a considerable component in the population of the city of Liverpool and the surrounding counties of Merseyside, Lancashire and Cheshire.

It is most fitting then that there should be a group of people in the city, most of whom are of Irish birth or descent and who are determined to mark the events of 1847-52 in a dignified and appropriate manner. The Great Famine Commemoration Committee (Liverpool) has members with roots in the four provinces of Ireland and is non-political and non-sectarian. A programme of lectures, exhibitions and other events has begun and plans are being laid for the establishment of a permanent memorial to those who passed through the city as migrants and to those who died here of famine-related disease in the years 1846-52. Eventually it is hoped to establish a Famine Trail marking the places in the city which were important to emigrants in the famine years. Those readers of *Familia* whose ancestors may well have passed through our city will be most welcome if, in years to come, they wish to visit this important stage in their Famine Forebears journey.

Ian McKeane is secretary of the *Great Famine Commemoration Committee* (Liverpool) and can be contacted c/o Liverpool Irish Centre, 127 Mount Pleasant, Liverpool L3 5TG, UK.

THE McGOOGINS OF ARMOY
A NORTH ANTRIM EMIGRANT FAMILY 1860-1890

by John H. McGuckin

Our ancestors of the nineteenth century were great correspondents. Letters containing family news sped back and forth across the Atlantic faster and more often than we imagine. Thousands of Irish immigrants sent news and money to those who remained in Ireland, often urging them to forsake the Old Country for the opportunities of the New World. Their relatives throughout Ireland reciprocated with lengthy descriptions of conditions on the family farm, in the local village.

Unfortunately, all too often the surviving portions of this correspondence are one-sided. Such is the case in a series of letters uncovered by Sherrill McGoogan of Portland, Oregon.[1] This article quotes extensively from these letters, which provide an interesting and at times moving vision of the life in the parish of Armoy in north County Antrim, in the last half of the nineteenth century. Supplemented by data drawn from research in American sources, these letters present a personal view of a family of Irish immigrants and those they left behind.

In 1888, two years before the last of the surviving letters was written, Armoy was described in George Henry Bassett's *Guide and Directory of Antrim* as 'a prettily situated village' about six miles south-west of Ballycastle. Located on the railroad from Ballycastle to Ballymoney, the land was 'fairly good' for dairy farming and tillage, with oats, potatoes and flax the principal crops. In 1881, the year after John McGoogan abandoned his farm, the village's population was 306.[2]

Although there were not any McGoogan families in Armoy in 1888, families with a surname pronounced something like 'McGoogan' had lived in this area of County Antrim since at least the reign of James I. On January 1, 1608, King James granted a pardon to a group of Irish rebels including men from Kilmachevet, County Antrim. Among those pardoned were Dionysius McGuiggin, Donell O Grougen and Eugene Crone McGyngen.[3] At the time of the Hearth Money Survey of 1663 in Armoy parish, John McGugin and Manus McGugin, probably brothers, lived in separate, but neighbouring, hearths.[4]

It is probable that these McGugins were descended from Scottish planters: MacGougan or MacGugan is a recognized Scottish surname,[5] and the McGoogans of Armoy were clearly Presbyterian. Still, there remains a possibility that the McGugins migrated to County Antrim from other, neighbouring counties of Ulster. 'McGugin' stems from a Gaelic linguistic root which was anglicized into numerous variants in Ireland, including McGoogan and McGuckin[6]. Several recorded McGuckins lived in Antrim in 1663, Murt McGuckian in Belfast and Daniel McGokan in Multas, near Larne.[7] It is possible that, during the Plantation era, some of the McGuckins who lived in and around Ballinderry parish in Counties Derry and Tyrone may have migrated from the western shore of Lough Neagh, across the River Bann, into Antrim. B.S. Turner suggests such a possibility for the McCaughans, another family living in Armoy parish.[8] However, whatever the resolution of this debate, it seems clear that the McGoogin family under consideration here stemmed, at least in the latter part of the eighteenth century, from John McClure McGoogan, who was born in Scotland.

After the 1663 survey the next reference to possible McGoogins in the neighbourhood of Armoy is found in the Flaxgrowers Bounty Lists of the Irish Linen Board (copy available in the PRONI). Prepared in 1796, the survey lists Hugh and James McGoogin in the nearby parish of Loughguile. Neal Mecaughan lived in Armoy.

The Tithe Applotment Survey for Armoy parish, taken in 1831, evidences seven McGoogan holdings in the parish. The largest tenancy was held by John McGoogan of Crockathenagh. His 31-acre farm, valued at more than £11, had formerly belonged to Patrick McGoogan, who was probably his deceased father, Alexander McGoogan, perhaps a brother or an uncle, lived on an 11-acre farm in the same townland. Other McGoogans lived nearby: Brian McGoogan had a 10-acre farm in the townland of Altcrinagh, James McGougan a 3-acre parcel in Ballybregagh and Duncan McGoogan a 6-acre parcel in Balleny. John McGoogan farmed 8 acres in Ballykinver, in addition perhaps, to another 8 acres in the same townland formerly leased to J. Montgomery. This second farm was listed in the survey as being held by 'J McGoogan'.

By the time of the Valuation Survey in the early 1860s, there had been major consolidation among the McGoogan holdings. Only two members of the family still leased land in Armoy parish; the other McGoogan families had either died in the Famine or migrated. James McGoogan, who was probably James McGougan of Ballybregagh in 1831, leased the largest property of 50 acres and a house, valued at £31, from George Macartney in the townland of Knocknahinch. Nearby lived Andrew M'Googan, who can be identified from the correspondence as either James' brother or nephew. Andy leased a 'house' without an 'office' from Robert Smith.[9] In 1831, Andrew McGoogan lived on a ten-acre farm in Ballybregagh, Loughguile parish. Because he is not listed in the Griffith Valuation Survey of the 1860s either he or his son may have abandoned the farm and taken up residence close to the rest of the family in Armoy.

James McGoogan of Knocknahinch was born in Dumfries, Scotland, in 1786. We do not know when he came to Ireland or, in fact, whether he came from a family which migrated between the Scottish borderlands and the north of Ireland. He married Jane Campbell, who was born in Ireland, in 1793. She was the daughter of James Campbell and Mary McClure. The McClures were, of course, another prolific Ulster family.[10] Although family research indicates that Jane was born in Ireland, their oldest son, John McClure McGoogan, was born on November 3, 1821 in Dumfries, Scotland.

Two additional sons, Samuel Hugh and Hugh, were born during the 1820s, perhaps before James returned to Ireland to begin to farm in Armoy, During the Famine era, both the younger boys emigrated to the United States. The United States immigration records contain two records which, while not precisely on point, may be the two brothers. A Samuel McGuggan arrived in New York City on July 8, 1842, on board the *New Zealand*. He gave his age as 17, four years younger than Samuel McGoogan of Knocknahinch would have been. Hugh McGugan, age 20, arrived from Belfast in New York City on the *Charlotte* on July 28, 1848.

Whether or not these immigration records are the McGoogan brothers, Samuel undoubtedly sent for his younger brother, who followed him to Pittsburgh, Pennsylvania. There both of them found work in the coal mines. Hugh married a woman named Nancy shortly after he arrived in America. By the time of the first of the surviving letters from Knocknahinch in 1860, he had three daughters: Jane, born in 1851/2, Sarah in 1855/6 and Mary in 1857/8.

Samuel married Almira Ann Christy of Pittsburgh on February 5, 1857. Almira had been born in Pennsylvania, probably in Pittsburgh. During the 1860 census, she gave her age as 30, putting her birthdate in 1829/30, making her only 17 or 18 years old when she married Samuel and only a year older when their son James Campbell was born on July 8, 1858. In Ireland, the oldest McGoogan son, John McClure, lived with his parents on the family farm in Knocknahinch.

This, then, was the McGoogan family when, on February 28, 1860, John wrote to Samuel, enclosing a draft for £11 sterling. One pound of the remittance was from their mother for her namesake, Hugh's daughter Jane. The balance was to repay funds which Samuel had sent home to sustain their father through an undefined crisis. John wrote, 'What we send to you we do not look upon as a present at all but as part of your own which you sent my Father when he had need of it.'

The money was derived from the sale of 21 pounds of pork at the 'great' market fair held in nearby Ballymoney on the first and third Thursday of each month. Sending the draft through an Antrim bank to a Pittsburgh correspondent had occasioned some trouble and several trips to Ballymoney to arrange. Correspondent banking was in its infancy in the mid-nineteenth century, as John McGoogan discovered. Not until 1871 did the American and British governments sign a postal-money-order agreement which would facilitate sending funds across the Atlantic.[11]

In 1860, however, John's local branch bank could not send money directly to Pittsburgh. In addition, he wrote, 'They told me that the main bank only corresponds with the main bank in a foreign country'. This meant a bank in New York City. John was not quite sure how Samuel would get the money from the New York bank. 'But, I suppose, and I hope, that as New York is a mercantile metropolis, there will be a branch in Pittsburgh where you may get it [the draft] cashed.'

Having disposed of his financial business, John proceeded to provide his brother with a farmer's overview of conditions in north

Antrim in early 1860. Six inches of snow covered the ground, delaying any farming that season. With some pride, John informed his brother that the farm had twelve head of cattle and two horses. Given the advanced and prolonged winter, he was concerned about feeding them since 'the cry for fodder through the county is truly awful'. Although the McGoogans seemed to have enough to see them to spring, John wrote that straw was selling at five shillings per measure and hay 'at anything you like to ask'.

John wrote again on August 17, 1861, in response to a letter from Samuel, who had asked for money himself this time. John simply could not help, although 'my heart is sore for your distress'. John's response to his brother's plea contained a mixture of hope for the future and caution about the present. He wrote that the previous year's crop had been a bad one, yielding only three bags of corn, which he had exchanged for flour. Although the 1861 crop promised to be 'excellent' and the flax harvest was 'the best we have had since I came home we have had to purchase our meal all this summer, and our rent is now due'. Further, his nine acres in corn looked 'remarkably well, as also our potato'.

At the end of the season, 'we will be able to help you a little', he promised. But, he cautioned that the abundant flax crop was a provincial phenomenon, reducing prices. Borrowing to help his American brothers was impossible. The local Armoy shopkeepers were receiving 'scarce any cash' and were obliged to 'give all on credit', a further hint as to John's shortage of ready cash.

This letter contains two interesting pieces of information about John himself. First, he writes that the flax harvest was the best 'since I came home'. This indicates that he, too, had left the family farm at some time, but later returned. By 1861, his father James was already 75 years old and it is natural to assume that John, as the oldest son, may have emigrated and then returned during the 1850s to take care of his ageing parents and the family farm.

The unanswerable question is whether John returned to his native Scotland for temporary work or, like his younger brothers, immigrated to America. A John McGoogin, age 27, arrived in New York City from Liverpool, on 11 May, 1846, on the *Atlas*. With him was Ann McGoogan, also aged 27 and, therefore, more likely his wife than his sister. Was this John, following his brother Samuel to America? Again, the ages do not quite match. John McClure was 25, not 27, in 1846. We may never know.

The second piece of personal information is more definite. On 14 August 1861, John married Mary Tait, 'a fine tall comely girl, about 23 years of age and,' John added somewhat proudly, 'that is considered very young in this country' (John, himself was 40!). Mary was the daughter of Hugh Tait of Ballyoregaugh and his wife Jane Armour and was born in Armoy in about 1839. In the practical way of farmers, John wrote to his brothers, 'She gets no fortune at present, but she is of most respectable people and [our] father and mother are both very fond of her, and I am as happy as you could wish.' John closed this letter filled with momentous news with the hope that, despite his financial difficulties, Samuel could continue to send the weekly American newspaper back to Knocknahinch, perhaps another hint that John may have, at one time, been in America himself.

The next letter is addressed to Samuel in Fayette, Pennsylvania, a small town in the coal country south of Pittsburgh. It is undated, but must have been written during the summer of 1862 because it announced the birth of James Campbell McGoogan (the namesake of Samuel's own son born in 1858) on 21 May and his christening on 13 July. The letter also includes family news about various relatives still in Ireland. Unfortunately, John's letter does not provide any guidance about the exact relationship of these relatives or whether they were McGoogans, Campbells or McClures.

A relative named John Morgan had died, although his relationship to the McGoogans is unknown. Uncle George died on 14 July, 1862 and was buried on the 16th of that month. Uncle Andrew, perhaps Andrew McGoogan who lived nearby in Knocknahinch, parish of Armoy, and his wife were well. John then provided updates on several other relatives, who may have been Andrew's children. Hugh was a chief boatman in the Coast Guard, John and Ruth were at home, 'Young Andy is, as ever, working at a hundred trades' and the 'rest are in America'.

The next surviving letters were written more than a decade later, in 1878. The 1870 American census tells us that, in the meantime, there had been many changes in the McGoogan households in Fayette.

Both Samuel and Hugh were interviewed by the census takers in June-July 1870. Each brother gave his age as 40, although their wives were more honest.

Hugh McGoogan lived with his family in Wilkins Township in Fayette County, Pennsylvania. He apparently rented his house because he did not, in response to a question on the census, claim to own any real property. His wife Nancy gave her age as 47. She had been born in Pennsylvania and kept house. Their six children all lived at home: three of the older daughters, Sarah, Mary and Rebecca, were in school. James, the only son, was born in 1861/2 and Nancy was born in 1866/7. Hugh's oldest daughter, Jane, lived nearby in Wilkins Township with the John Morrow family as a domestic servant. Morrow was a farmer and Jane helped his wife Sarah take care of their two children, Olivia, age 3, and Benjamin, age 2.

Brother Samuel lived in nearby Sedickley Township and claimed that he owned real estate valued at $800 and personal property worth $100. Almira gave her age as 30 and, like Nancy, she kept house. James Campbell, their oldest son, was in school with his brother, John McClure, born on August 20, 1861, and sister Margaret Ann, born on 18 April, 1864. The baby of the family, Elizabeth Jane, born on 12 May, 1867, was at home. Sam's mother-in-law Elizabeth Christy, age 69, lived with them.

John's next letter to his brother Samuel is dated 17 February, 1878. The Irish branch of the family had changed during the intervening years as well. The letter reports the death of their father James, in his nineties, on 11 February, 1878, after a three-week illness, 'sensible to the last'. The burial took place on 13 February. James had died with John at his side. John wrote, '[F]or the space of 5 or 6 hours before his departure he prayed all the time and I prayed with him and we sang a psalm to him.'

The letter also discloses that Jane Campbell McGoogan had died at some time before 21 July, 1877, when John's daughter Ellen was born. By this time, John and Mary McGoogan had had eight children in 15 years. James Campbell was born on 21 May, 1862, Samuel McClure on 3 October, 1863, John on 1 November, 1865, Hugh on 22 March, 1868, Mary Jane on 28 February, 1871, Margaret Anne on 13 April, 1873, George on 31 July, 1874, and Ellen in 1877.

James, the family patriarch, could not have died at a worse time. John wrote, 'I have to tell you that we are all but broke and I fear very much we will have to sell out. This last year was a very bad one. There was almost no crops at all of any kind by reason of the continual rains'. He solicited his brother's advice on whether to emigrate or not. 'I am in great trouble,' he confided, but he estimated that he would clear a hundred pounds if he sold his leasehold to the farm. Nonetheless, he was worried that this would not be sufficient to bring him and his large family to America. By July, 1878, when he wrote again, John had decided 'to try another year or two'. In a lengthy letter, dated 24 July, 1878, he responded to a letter from Fayette dated 6 July. The mail was surprising fast between Ireland and the United States in the 1870s

John described to his brother something of his life on the family farm in north Antrim. As in many Irish families, John had known little about the family's business affairs while his parents were alive. In fact, it appears that his mother handled all the bills and kept them secret from both her husband and her son. Life had been hardly easy for the eldest son, living with his aged parents. He told his brothers in America,

> I must tell you that whilst [our] parents lived they would have everything their own way. There was nothing for me but work and for the last 9 or 10 years servants' wages grew so high and servants grew so impudent that for at least the last years they [John and Jane] would have none of them but you could not expect that a farm such as ours could be laboured as it required with so little help.

Adhering to his parents' wishes, John refused to hire servants to help him on the farm, waiting until his sons were old enough to work in the fields. The price he had to pay for domestic tranquility with his parents was that 'all the labor devolved on me and my children were kept from school to assist me in such light work as they were able for.'

Once Jane McGoogan died and her son finally looked 'into the state of affairs,' he determined to break a firm family rule and borrow. It is hard to determine from John's letter if his father understood what he was doing. John clearly saw disaster staring his family in the face. When the bills came due, they were 'heavier than I was aware of,' he told his brother. Creditors had to be paid and John faced the classic farmer's dilemma: '.. to meet them [the bills] or part of the stock had to be sold reducing the means of making money'. Then, some of the remaining livestock died and the house was 'falling into decay'.

Eventually, John confronted his father with the sorry state of the family's affairs and obtained his permission to borrow. John unsuccessfully approached several sources, including, one presumes, the two banks which were doing business in Ballymoney. Alexander McGugan was cashier of the Ulster Bank branch in Church Street in 1888 and he may have already held this position a decade earlier. If so, he declined to assist his kinsman.

John eventually borrowed £160 at 6% per annum from an attorney in Ballymoney, whom he identifies as agent for the Antrim estate. In 1888, A. McDonald held this post and either he or his predecessor made the loan against the McGoogan tenancy. Like most lenders, he took a healthy percentage of the loan principal, totalling £15, as the costs for making the loan. James assigned his tenant-right to his son John, who, in turn, gave a mortgage on it to the attorney. After all costs were paid, John had little more than £145 left. He used part of the balance to buy three cows , three springing heifers and fifty slates with nails to repair the roof of the house The heifers cost between £9 and £10, 'a very high price' in John's opinion. Fortunately, all three heifers dropped female calves, 'which I look upon as a piece of good fortune and a blessing from God.'

Despite all this, John would have emigrated if his father had not lingered so long in his last illness. Now, the dutiful son felt the pressure to redeem his enormous loan before leaving Ireland. His older boys, who were opposed to leaving Armoy, were capable and willing to work on the farm and the inconvenience of taking the younger children ('who would be very troublesome to take abroad,' according to their father) to America counselled against the long journey.

Personal sorrows and troubles added to John's financial woes. His ten-year-old son Hugh had died suddenly on 21 March, 1875, and John himself had lost the hearing in one ear as the result of a cold which led to complications. He wrote to Samuel that he felt himself to be 'failing' and, then, with the resignation and sense of acceptance typical of many Irish farmers, concluded with:

> But what are all the troubles of this life, which is but short, if we have accepted the salvation offered through our Redeemer. We shall despise them all trusting that we will soon attain to a life of perfect happiness where no trouble can assail or any danger affright.

In the meantime, John McGoogan was not Samuel's only correspondent. In late July, 1879, he received a letter dated 14 July from his cousin and namesake Samuel McClure from Yuba City in Sutter County, in the California Gold Country. Samuel McClure was undoubtedly related through Samuel's grandmother Mary McClure. He describes himself by the all-purpose term, 'a cousin'. Samuel was a popular name among the Antrim McClures and it is even more difficult to trace this cousin through the American immigration records than it is to identify the McGoogans.

Three Samuel McClures arrived in New York during the Famine era. Two of these men arrived with their wives and children. A third arrived with his brothers and sisters. Samuel McClure, age 18, arrived on May 6, 1848, on the *New Zealand*, the same ship which had brought Samuel McGuggan to America in 1842. Travelling with him were his siblings William, a wood ranger, age 35, who headed the group as far as the immigration authorities were concerned; Betty, age 36; another William, age 22, who may have been a brother or a cousin; Mary Jane, age 17; and Eliza, age 17.[12] Because Samuel McClure told his cousin that his family was scattered across the United States in Michigan and New York, where a sister Jane lived, it is tempting to think that he was a member of this large family which arrived together in 1848. His letters refer to sisters Sarah and Mary and a brother John who remained in Ireland.

Two Samuel McClures appear in the 1860 census for California, one lived in Sierra County and one in Siskiyou County. A Samuel McClure does not appear in the 1870 California census. However, the 1884-1885 Sutter County Directory lists him in Yuba City living on a ranch of 90 acres. He wrote in 1879 to reestablish contact with his cousin and to send along a picture of his youngest son. Samuel McClure married his wife L. J. Burnett in December, 1867. In 1881, he had two boys and two girls still living, another son, named after his own father, having died, aged 5, in 1873/74.

Shortly after Samuel McGoogan responded to Samuel McClure's letter, John McGoogan had another change of heart and determined to quit Ireland. On November 24, 1879, he wrote to Samuel announcing the imminent departure of the family, including his wife who was nearly eight months pregnant, for America. The arrival of some of his wife's Tait relatives from America, including two brothers who lived in Jersey City, New Jersey, had apparently led to lengthy conversations about immigration. 'They both came to us and encouraged us to clear out and go to America which I have done', John wrote. He sold the leasehold and planned to travel through New York City, planned to visit his Tait relatives and then travel to Fayette, where John hoped to find work. The excitement of the trip and the relief at having 'sold out' are apparent in John's letter. Since all his surviving children died in America, John had apparently persuaded his reluctant older sons to accompany him to Pennsylvania.

The New World held no relief for John McGoogan. He hoped to see his brother for the first time in decades at Christmas, 1879. He achieved this ambition and saw his son William born in Everson, Pennsylvania, on 11 January, 1880. There, John died on 26 April, 1880, aged 59. He left his widow Mary with a large family to support, close to the families of his two brothers. His brother Samuel's daughter Mary Malinda was born shortly thereafter on 5 April, 1880.

The news of John's death quickly reached Ireland via Samuel's correspondence. Samuel McClure, who had heard from his mother about John's death, sent his condolences from Yuba City in a letter dated 2 February, 1881. Samuel also remembered John fondly. He wrote, 'He was like a brother to me when I was a small boy and his kindness to me I never will never forget'. On 26 April, 1880, 'cousin' Andrew McGoogin wrote from Ballybregagh in Loughguile to mourn John, who was 'so upright and honest'.

Andy saw fit to let his relatives know that they were well rid of Ireland. He reported that 1880 was an even worse year than 1879. Although 'we have [a] warm dry summer', there was no work for the farms, a poor crop, no trade and no money anywhere. His own son James and his wife and eight children were barely scraping a living.

So many small farmers were close to bankruptcy and when the rent was due, many 'could not pay much more than one shilling in the pound'.

Samuel McClure was not having a better time of it in California. He wrote that continuous rain had broken the local levies, cut him off from the neighboring towns and flooded his entire farm, except for an acre or two. 'This is the worst time we have had for many a year,' he lamented. 'I cannot tell the amount of damage it has done...'. Like John before him, Samuel was thinking of selling 'as soon as I can find a buyer at any price and leaving here'. So desperate was he that he told his cousin that we would accept $30 an acre, half the price he had paid for his farm.

We do not know if Samuel actually sold his farm. He was still there in 1884. His next letter to Fayette was from Ballycraig in Antrim. He had accompanied his mother on a visit to the old parish and wrote on 30 July, 1890, to tell his American cousins that much had changed. He wrote,

> I passed the old home where you and I often plaid together it don't look much like the old home when your father and mother lived there There is a great change Well, there is so much change in Ireland, in every thing. It don't look like the same country to me.

Not the least of the changes was the result of better economic times for rural Ireland. Samuel wrote that money was now plentiful and the farmers were doing well. Houses were built throughout the country. 'Times is good and money is plenty. Men gets good pay here for all kinds of labour'. Rain was plentiful, but not destructive, and Sam thought the local crops looked good, He repeated many of these comments in a second letter, dated 22 December, 1890, but admitted, 'I like California a great deal better on account of the climate'.

With this the surviving correspondence ends. Several themes are apparent from these letters. First is the strong, continuing religious faith shared by both the McGoogans and the McClures. The death of James McGoogan, as described by his son, is an edifying scene and it is clear that John ascribed any good fortune to divine Providence. In 1861, he wrote to his brother, '....[I]f the Lord be pleased to send us a favorable harvest, we will have plenty of everything in a short time. ..' Despite his personal sorrows, he expressed a belief in the Lord's blessing, writing ' will not trouble you any more at present but to assure you that wife and family all join in love to you and yours and in praying for God's blessing upon us all...

His cousin Samuel McClure shared this solid faith. In 1881, he wrote to Sam McGoogan after John's death, urging him to submit to the will of God: 'in a short time we much all follow him to the last resting place.' In describing the floods which spelled financial ruin and the end of his California dream, Sam sounds exactly like John when he wrote, 'Dear Cousin, I have not time to write you one half what I would like to but thank God my family are all well.'

A second theme is evident, the strong feeling of family which bound this extended Antrim clan. The correspondence between the brothers and between the cousins is affectionate and warm in tone. Money clearly flowed back and forth across the Atlantic as it was needed and as it could be repaid. Information and newspapers were constantly exchanged both between Fayette and Armoy and between Yuba City and Fayette.

The separations caused by time and distance were keenly felt and family ties remained strong. In the mid-1870s Samuel McClure had obtained information about his McGoogan kinsmen from one of their cousins, H. McNeal, who showed up unexpectedly at the McClure ranch. McNeal stayed for part of a day, and 'left to bring his trunk to my house, but never returned.' Unimpressed by this lack of consideration, McClure did not respond to McNeal's later letters, but kept the information about the McGoogans and sought to see them when he next came east.

In his 1879 letter, Samuel McClure summarized an odyssey he had made in 1874, when he left California to visit friends in the east of the United States. He visited his sister Jane in New York, seeing her for the first time in twenty years. His aunt Mary's family lived in Rockland, Illinois, and, *en route*, his sister urged him to look up the McGoogans around Pittsburgh. Arriving on the morning Pennsylvania Central train in Pittsburgh and armed with Samuel's address from a friend or relative, William McMillin, he searched vainly throughout the day for a trace of Samuel McGoogan, 'but could not hear anything of you. So I left out of hart. I could only stay the one day as my wife had telegraphed for me to come home.'

Finally, life during the latter part of the nineteenth century was not any easier in America than in Antrim. Samuel McClure's perilous existence as a rancher in Sutter County, California, was no easier than his cousin John's hard life in Armoy. Their letters evidence a common concern for crops, lifestock and the weather. We do not have Samuel McGoogan's part of the correspondence, but the life he and his brother Hugh passed in the coal mines could not have been easy ones. Like many Irish immigrants of an earlier era, they could have written to their kinsmen, 'This America is not what it used to be', or 'any person who can make a fair living at home are better Stay theire'.[13] Still, they persevered. The correspondence summarized here remains a lasting testament to the determination and courage of those Irish men and women who left their native land to search for a better life.

NOTES

1. In preparing this article, the author acknowledges with gratitude the research provided by Ms McGoogan as part of her own research on her branch of the McGuckin Family.
2. G H Bassett, *The Book of Antrim, 1888* (reprinted edition Belfast, 1989) , p. 87
3. *Irish Patent Rolls,* James I (Dublin, 1966), p. 110
4. PRONI, Distribution of Family Names in the Glens and the Route, p. 14
5. F. Adams, *The Clans, Septs and Regiments of the Scottish Highlands* (Edinburgh, 1924), p 150
6. R. Bell, *The Book of Ulster Surnames* (Belfast, 1988), p.163.
7. 'Hearth Money Rolls,' *The Glynns,* vol. 5, p. 15 (1977).
8. B.S. Turner, 'The Surname MacCaughan in the North Antrim Glynns,' *The Glynns,* vol 12, p 15 (19 84). See also, Bell *Ulster Surnames,* p. 138
9. Interestingly, William McGuckian appears as a tenant in Drumadarragh in the Valuation Survey. He was probably not related to the McGoogans
10. See, for example, R.D. McClure, 'Serendipity and the Cracked Griddle: An Account of Research on the McClure Family,' *Familia* vol. 2, no. 10, p 72 (1994)
11. K A Miller, *Emigrants and Exiles, Ireland and the Irish Exodus to North America* (New York, 1985), p 357,
12. I A Glazier, ed., *Famine Immigrants,* vol. 6, p 447 (Baltimore, 1985)
13. Miller, *Emigrants and Exiles,* pp. 358-359

NINETEENTH-CENTURY RECORDS IN THE ARCHIVES OF THE ROYAL VICTORIA HOSPITAL

by R. S. J. Clarke

The Archives Office of the Royal Victoria Hospital is situated in the King Edward Building and has built up a valuable collection of material dating back to the opening of the first Dispensary and Fever Hospital in 1797. This became the Belfast General Hospital in 1848, the Belfast Royal Hospital in 1875 and the Royal Victoria Hospital in 1899. The material contents had clearly been accumulating over many years but the first Honorary Archivist was Dr R. S. Allison who took on the post after retiring from his post of Consultant Neurologist in 1964. He was followed by Dr H. G. Calwell in 1978, Dr J. S. Logan in 1986 and myself in 1993. All have built up the archives in terms of the actual records and they have produced a stream of papers and books on the history of the hospital and medicine generally.

For reasons of space the archivists have decided only to collect material on paper and have resisted the temptation to turn the room into a hospital museum; only in exceptional circumstances, when precious objects were liable to be destroyed, have they been taken into the Archives Office.

The great majority of the material relates to (1) the history and activities of the above hospitals, with (2) some material on the history of related hospitals, the Throne, ophthalmic and the Benn. Other material (3) relates to the medical students and medical staff of the hospitals. There is very little archival material relating to nursing and other staff until this century and even then not as much as there should be.

The Belfast General and the Belfast Royal Hospitals
Probably the most prized possessions of the Archives Office are the two *Royal Charters*. The first, dated 3 March 1875, is handwritten on three pages of parchment, the first of which has lithographed decoration and a portrait of Queen Victoria. It has the Royal Seal on wax, 6 inches in diameter. It establishes the corporate entity to be

known as The Belfast Royal Hospital. The second or Revised Charter also consists of three handwritten pages of parchment, all with lithographed decoration and the portrait, and a similar seal. It is dated 16 January 1899 and establishes the corporate entity know as The Royal Victoria Hospital.

The most convenient and accessible record is the collection of *Annual Reports* of the above hospitals from 1818-1948. These are much more than just descriptions of the hospital activities for they give a vivid picture of the health and social conditions in Belfast over the years. The early years up to about 1850 are largely concerned with 'fever', a broad term for four different conditions all recognised to be contagious. For instance, the 1832 epidemic of cholera is highlighted, as is the Great Famine of 1845-6-7 with the burden placed on the hospital. The Annual Report with its Surgical Report gives details of the operations carried out, at least in some years. One learns that there were a steady number of operations even before the advent of anaesthesia, such as excision of the elbow joint in 1843.

The first record of anaesthesia is in the report covering 1849-50 and in the next year the purchase of chloroform cost £1 4s 0d. The names of the physicians, surgeons, apothecaries and committee members over the years are listed, as well as many of the doctors who looked after dispensary districts over the city. Of wider interest are the lists of subscribers throughout the city, published street by street until 1848. Since these comprised most of the citizens of Belfast, they are a supplement to the street directories, though they don't give house numbers. One unusual record is the names and deaths, age, date and cause of death of 30 patients in 1824-5 and 1825-6 but sadly this was not continued. For instance there was Rose Barber, died 27 January 1825 of typhus – speechless, insensible when admitted from Malone; and Robert Patterson, aged 50 ill [from fever] for 3 days admitted 21 April 1825, died 7 May 1825.

The hospital *Minute Books* from 1822 -1948 were discovered and preserved by Dr H. G. Calwell and contribute a valuable day to day record of hospital activities. There are 18 folio volumes for the last century, all handwritten but clear and giving detail of income and expenditure, appointments, building maintenance and many names and dates of patients admissions and discharges. For instance, at a meeting on 18 December 1831 it is resolved that ' Samuel Dyer [be] admitted for two weeks; Sam Sands do one month; Wm. Hanna do two weeks.' They are, however not indexed and are of limited use to family historians.

Another collection is the *Medical Staff Minutes* (2 volumes pre 1900) and *Reports* (2 volumes) dating from 1865. The former are more detailed accounts of the meetings and the latter appear to report the decisions of the staff on matters of hospital policy. For instance in June 1883 there is a 'Report from Dr Ross that the proximity of the Delirium Tremens Ward to the Fever patients disturbed the rest of the latter. The staff cannot at present see any remedy.....'. The Minutes contain much detail about the duties and teaching of the medical students and in September 1889 there is a Report that 'The staff having received an application from a Lady student to be admitted to the practice of the Hospital wards, they see no reason why the application should be refused'. Both Minutes and Reports contain much detail about day to day nursing problems and in fact are probably the main source of detail on nursing practice and regulations in the hospital. The question of where consumption was to be managed in the 1880s was aired, along with Mr Forster Green's offer of £5,000. In 1883 the use of beds in the Throne Hospital was considered the best solution and this appears to have been an interim measure until the Forster Green Hospital was opened in 1895.

There is a collection of folio-size *Scrapbooks* or Newspaper Cutting Albums dating back to 1848. Those for the last century are 1) 1848-1872; 2)1872-1882 and 3)1887-1901 and there are a further 12 similar volumes covering this century together with smaller collections donated to Archives at random. The early volumes consist mainly of reports of the annual and quarterly management meetings together with medical reports. There are also, however, advertisements for posts of doctors, nurses and housekeepers and notices relating to the street by street collections, Sunday Collections, and donations and bequests. There are rules regarding the work and training of the doctors and nurses and rules regarding admission of patients. Only occasionally is there a hint of controversy as occurred over the appointment of hospital chaplains in December 1875. A particularly interesting group of reports in 1876 (not often found) contains details of accidents from the daily papers when the patients were admitted to the hospital. They include a report of the death of and inquest on William Johnston who fell out of 'a car', probably owing to its jolting. An unusual report is of 'a man named James Crilly was knocked down last night about 11 o'clock in Little Donegall Street by a soldier and sustained such injuries as necessitated his removal to the Royal Victoria Hospital. A policeman who saw the occurrence arrested the soldier and lodged him in the Police Office.' More typical are the reports of one Mary McLean, a middle-aged woman who sustained burns from falling into the fire during an epileptic fit and of John Brown who fell off a ladder while painting a house.

There is also a parallel collection of two quarto Honorary Secretary's *Minute Books* 1863-1870 and 1871-1877. They contain some handwritten minutes for the earlier years but are mainly newspaper cuttings of public meetings and add little to the other books. On the purely financial side there are *Account Books* for 1871-1876 and 1876-1880. They include details of salaries and wages paid and purchases for all the little items required by the hospital such as coal, insurance, food, furniture, medicines, cutlery and blacking for ranges.

There are two volumes covering the *Finance Committee Minutes* for the last century of 1880-1883, 1884-1901 and a run has survived since that date. (The first of these also includes other committees). The information is largely routine, though there are items such as 'Mr McGinty refuses to collect amounts due by Pay Patients unless he is paid a special commission, which is a new departure (June 1900). It is clear form this and other passages that collecting the money for the running of the hospital was by no means an easy task.

Minutes and accounts for the scheme known as the *Hospital Saturday* exist from its inception in 1884. Unlike the lists of subscribers in the Annual Repots they give only the names of collectors and collection stations, together with the amounts raised. There are printed Annual Reports of the Hospital Saturday but they go back only as far as 1902.

The *Hospital Sunday* or Charity Sermon was a means of raising funds from the beginning of the hospital. However, by 1886 it had apparently become ineffective and a committee of the clergy of Belfast was set up. It cannot have been very effective either and was in competition with the Hospital Saturday scheme. At all events only 9 meetings are recorded before 1905, after which there were no further meetings.

Another record which is of interest as the centenary of the Royal Victoria approaches is the minute book on the *New Hospital Scheme* from the first meeting in 1896. Much of the volume is concerned with the mundane matter of fund raising but includes reports on the proposed sites, the revision of of the Charter, choice of architect and detailed plans. Again and again we see the signature of William J. Pirrie (later Lord Pirrie) who chaired various committees in connection with the project and, with his wife, played a large part in its funding. The volume concludes with the settling of outstanding accounts and thanking William Pirrie in 1904.

There is an alphabetical record of the *Life Governors* of the hospital from the expanded scheme of 1864 to the last entry in 1916. Addresses are recorded in most instances but often only in broad terms such as Whitehouse, Holywood or even Belfast. The scheme had been introduced in 1852 to encourage wealthy and influential people to subscribe £50 or more in one sum, so it is included here under the financial umbrella.

The Throne Hospital

In 1872 Mr John Martin of Shrigley, County Down, gave 28 acres of land near Belfast for building a Convalescent Children's Hospital. Other funds were soon received and the Throne Hospital was opened in August 1876 and it was extended to include adults in the following year. The early Minute Books of the hospital have survived from 1880-1894 and 1896-1916. In addition there are minutes of the 'Consumptive Committee' of the hospital from 1886 when plans to open wards for patients with tuberculosis in the Throne Hospital were first discussed. It appears to have ceased to function in 1909. The hospital was always administered as an annex of the Royal Victoria Hospital and Annual Reports of the Throne Hospital are included in the Royal Victoria Hospital Annual Reports from 1876.

The Ophthalmic and Benn Hospitals

The first of these specialist hospitals to be built in Belfast was the ophthalmic Hospital in Great Victoria Street which opened on 1 January 1868. The early records of this are lost but a Minute Book starting in 1893 has survived. The book covers the period up to 1921 and includes much detail of the small donations and expenditure. However, there are references to weightier matters and in 1911 certainly there were problems of apparent inaccuracies in payment of the accounts.

The Benn or Ulster Eye, Ear and Throat Hospital opened in 1874 and again one of its old Minute Books, covering 1897-1929 has been saved in the Archives Office. This volume contains exclusively minutes without all the details of cash transactions. For instance on 26 October 1898 'Doctor McKeown be instructed to get the Electric light as per Mr W H Drennan's letter at the cost not exceeding fifteen pounds'. Perhaps in connection with this 'blinds in the female ward had been put up'. Both these hospitals have been closed and since many of the medical staff were also associated with the Royal Victoria Hospital, it seemed appropriate to take some of the records there for storage.

Students, Medical Staff and Nurses
Details of the earlier *Medical Students* are not preserved though many references to them occur in the Medical Staff Minutes. However, later, a full Student Register is preserved, the first volume running from 1866 to 1916. It records the names, together with hospital year and college year, a short address, date of entry, fees paid and other notes. The first entry in 1866 is of Mr John Walton Browne, son of Mr Samuel Browne, a surgeon of the hospital who was later to give the opening address for the new building in 1903. One striking observation in the early years is the spread of home addresses including on the first page Castlederg, Banbridge, Portglenone, Newton-Limavady, Broughshane, Dungiven, Randalstown, Killyleagh, Saintfield etc. etc. This valuable volume had been deteriorating but fortunately it has been strengthened and conserved so that it is now easily consulted.

There is a large collection of class certificates as well as testimonials and graduation and post-graduate diplomas (totalling about 30 in all) of Dr John Redmond of Loughgall who qualified with the Society of Apothecaries, London in 1881. These documents are interesting for the signatures of noted Physicians and Surgeons of the Belfast hospitals and beyond, also for the decorative quality of formal documents, the finest of all being that of the Apothecaries Society (59 x 44 cms). They also prove that paper work and bureaucracy is not an invention of the twentieth century.

Smaller groups of original and photocopied certificates are also preserved for Dr James Gibson (c. 1854), Dr Andrew George Malcolm (MD Edinburgh 1842), James Coyne (LAR Dublin 1864) and Dr James McCleery (LRCS Dublin 1847). The material on Dr Malcolm includes a large number of his original letters and publications as well as photocopies, all collected for his biography by Dr Hugh Calwell.

Among the nineteenth-century busts, portraits and photographs in the Archives office and nearby rooms are busts of Dr James McDonnell and Sir William MacCormac of the medical staff and James Girdwood, Hospital Treasurer. There are portraits of Queen Victoria, Professor James Cumming, Dr Andrew Marshall, Dr S S Thomson, Sir Thomas Houston, Dr Henry Murney, Mr James Barron, and Viscount Pirrie. In addition, there are reproductions of these and photographs of most of the great figures of the hospital in albums in the Archives office. There are also group photographs of the Resident Medical Staff from 1891 onwards.

One of the most useful records in the office is the collection of miscellaneous items relating to all visiting or consultant medical staff of the hospital from its beginnings. It is, of course, very patchy in its contents and while it contains much about the more conspicuous figures such as Dr Andrew Malcolm, Mr James Moore, (surgeon and artist), and Sir William Whitla, it contains little about such figures as Dr Henry Forcade who was a prominent surgeon from 1819 until he died in 1835. Much information has also been collected about other doctors in Northern Ireland such as Dr Samuel Black of Newry, a pioneer cardiologist who lived in Marcus Square 1819-1832 and is buried in St Patrick's Churchyard. It is salutary to recall that figures such as Dr Samuel Black and Dr William Drennan were practising in Newry at the beginning of the last century and were at least as noteworthy as any in Belfast.

The archives office has collected also a working library of material relating to Belfast and medical history generally. Perhaps more unusual is the collection of books written by medical staff which, of course, is particularly numerous in the present century. Those of the past century include, Dr J. S Drennan's *Poems and Sonnets* (1895); Professor Alexander Gordon's *Treatise on the Fractures of the Lower End of the Radius* (1875); Dr James Lindsay's *Climatic Treatment of Consumption* (1887); Henry MacCormac's *Consumption* (1865); Sir William MacCormac's *Notes and Recollection of an Ambulance Surgeon* (1871); and Sir William Whitla's many writings on pharmacy and therapeutics.

Finally, there are notes on other notable personalities connected with the hospital, such as Ann Marshall who was appointed Head Nurse in 1832 and died in 1860. Of other nurses in the last century we know virtually nothing but with Miss Mary Frances Bostock, who was appointed Matron of the Throne Hospital in 1887 and of the Royal Victoria in 1901, we move into an era of detailed Minutes of committees and testimonials as to her work.

In conclusion, we are fortunate in having so much compared with many similar institutions. This is partly owing to the pioneer work of Dr Andrew Malcolm who wrote his *History of the General Hospital, Belfast* in 1851 and thus created a climate of interest. Credit must also go to the foresight of the administrators of the hospital who set aside an archives office and secretary away from the covetous eyes of the clinicians who might want both for themselves. Finally we must be grateful to Dr Sidney Allison, Dr Hugh Calwell and Dr John Logan who have continued to build up the collection with contemporary and historic material.

THE LILLEY FAMILY OF KILWARLIN, CO. DOWN

by J. Fred Rankin

Herbert Robert Lilley was born in Belfast on 28 October 1886, the second son of Samuel and Eliza Lilley; he married Margaret Marion Stuart at May Street Presbyterian Church on 25 August 1925. He died on 20 April 1970. They had two children, Kathleen, born 17 July 1928, who became the author's wife, and Brian, born 5 May 1931.

Bertie, as he was known in the family, showed considerable artistic talent at an early age and found employment in the linen industry, becoming Head Designer of Robert McBride & Co.Ltd., Ormeau Avenue, Belfast, makers of fine linen and damask. He was also a painter of considerable achievement, spending his holidays before the first world war painting in various European countries. His holiday travels took him to Bruges in Belgium, to northern France, to the Bordeaux area of western France and to northern Spain whilst he was a frequent visitor on business to St Gall in Switzerland as well as to Belgium and France. He won a scholarship to the South Kensington Art School and his work was exhibited, not only locally but at the Hibernian Academy in Dublin, the Walker Art Gallery in Liverpool and in Glasgow. He was a prominent member of the Ulster Arts Club and, from papers in the family's possession, it is clear that he enjoyed the company and the friendship of the foremost artists of the day. He was also a part-time lecturer in white embroidery and linen design in the early days of the Municipal Technical Institute in Belfast.

Apart from two brothers and one sister, he spoke little about his ancestry and, over recent years, Kathleen and I have spent a considerable amount of time and effort in piecing together a family tree. We were anxious to trace, if possible, an ancestral source for this artistic talent, or perhaps it was a product of the period in which he was brought up, when the linen industry was one of the major sources of employment in east Ulster. Kathleen remembered being taken, as a child, to a grave in the City Cemetery, where his father, who had died relatively young, and mother were buried. Apart from that, there was a vague notion that the family had come from the area beyond Hillsborough, Co.Down; the townland of Taughblane in the parish of Hillsborough rang some bells with other members of the family.

This was not a lot of information to go on but it was at least a start. The first task was to trawl all the church registers of every denomination in the Hillsborough area in the Public Record Office of Northern Ireland. We also had an initial run through the early registers for Lisburn Cathedral; this latter register yielded the burial of Joseph Lilly at Blaris on 3.2.1722/3. The parish church of Hillsborough yielded a vast number of Lilleys, being baptised, being married or being buried. There were also some eighteenth-century vestry minutes which included a list of land holders in the parish; in 1764 William Lilley occupied 8 acres in Toghblane (modern spelling, Taughblane).

Here was a point in time from which we could come forward and go backwards. The registers of the two Kilwarlin parish churches, Hillsborough Presbyterian church, Kilwarlin Moravian church all yielded Lilleys, showing that intermarriage with other families spread the family around varying denominations. We now had a large quantity of names, the problem was to put them together; at the beginning, we had nothing earlier than 1764 and all these Lilleys seemed to have been descended from William of Toghblane. The name was sufficiently uncommon to discard the possibility that another Lilley might have settled in the district. As far as possible, all the burial entries in the registers were checked in the relevant graveyards, but this exercise raised another problem. It was found that some headstone inscriptions did not have related entries in the burial registers; this appeared to come about when the parish churchyard was the 'accustomed' burial place for all denominations, in fact, before the other churches were built. It seemed that while other denominations might be buried in the churchyard, they were not necessarily entered in the burial register. It pays to check both! We also found another Lilley family buried in Broomhedge parish churchyard, which was duly noted but the registers were not checked in that case as, by then, we were working on the fringes of the 'core' family.

At this point, we started looking for other corroborative sources to help tie all these names together and we decided to study the Downshire Kilwarlin estate records. The Downshire estates are extremely well documented and the family historian who studies these is richly blessed. We found that William, a wheelwright, took out a lease of 8 acres in Toghblane in 1756, the lease to run for three lives, the natural life of the said William Lilly, of Joseph Lilly, his eldest son aged 12 years and of William Lilly, his third son, aged 8 years and during the life of the longest liver of them. This lease did not expire until 5 January 1823. In the Hillsborough parish vestry book, in the year 1788 the road in Toghblane was to be repaired 'between Joseph Lilly and the Big Hill'. This would suggest that William was by then dead and the farm was being run by his eldest son Joseph. It also tells us that young William, the third son, died on 5 January 1823.

However, by following the estate maps, which were drawn at regular intervals, together with the actual leases and rental books, as well as Griffith's Valuation of 1861 and valuation maps, we were able to trace the handing down and division of these 8 acres virtually until the present day. Some of the older nearby residents remember the Lilleys of Taughblane, who seemed to have died out about fifty years ago. (There are still several Lilley families in the Kilwarlin district, but none, as far as I can tell, on the ancestral land in Taughblane.) Imagine my delight when I called on the modern bungalow on the corner of Ballygowan Road and Gulf Lane/ Corcreeny Road to enquire if there was any knowledge of the Lilley family, to be told that this corner was still known as Lilley's corner and the occupant of this modern bungalow had never known the reason! Small wonder in that three of the four corners were occupied by Lilleys a century ago! In fact, what was apparently the Lilley homestead was now no more than a stone wall in the middle of the fields. We now had enough material to put together a family tree spanning the late eighteenth and early nineteenth centuries; the problem was to work backwards from our own time to connect it.

Bertie's father was Samuel; the headstone in the City Cemetery informed us that he died on 14 January 1898, aged 48 and that his wife, Eliza Jane, had died on 28 January 1922 aged 61. There were also two children who died in infancy. The address given in the newspaper notice was 261 Albertbridge Road; in the street directories prior to his death he was listed as a salesman. We know from family papers that he worked for John Robb and Co of Castle Place. We also know that he moved to Albertbridge Road from 107 Peter's Hill; in the 1884 and 1887 directories that address lists Campbell & Lilley, drapers. Possibly Campbell pulled out of the partnership and Samuel took a job with John Robb around 1890. It is of interest that Bertie's elder brother was called William Edwin Campbell, although he was known in the family as Eddie. No doubt the Campbell came from father's partner; there also appears to have been a tradition throughout the generations to call the first born son William.

At this stage, Kathleen said that although her mother was Presbyterian and they were married in a Presbyterian church, her father had always said that his family was Methodist. Methodist records were not so plentiful, so where to start? In PRONI, we found a volume of registers of the Lisburn Circuit, embracing all the 'classes' in that circuit. This turned out to be a rich source of detail which enabled us to go back two more generations. Not only were we able to find Samuel's birth in 1850 as well as his seven brothers and sisters, but also his father and mother, Robert and Jane. On Jane's death in 1865, Robert married again and had two further daughters; on that wife's death he married a third time before his own death in 1889, after which his third wife married again! This took some sorting out. As well as the church register, we obtained copies of the actual certificates from Joyce House in Dublin, where we trawled the indexes from the commencement of civil registration in 1864 until 1900. This trawl produced Samuel's marriage certificate; he was married on 10 October 1882, a draper of 107 Peter's Hill, to Eliza Jane Wilson, daughter of Joseph Wilson, car owner of Strandtown. They were married in University Road Methodist Church; we have never found out why University Road was chosen as neither lived in the area, perhaps it was fashionable at that time.

The Lisburn Methodist register contained other vital information. It listed the members of each 'class' every year from 1833 until 1894, just the span of years in which we were interested. In 1833, Robert and Jane were at Upper Maze, gradually other members of the family and their own children were listed. They moved through Ballykeel Artifinny to Ballyknock and finally to Lower Magheragall in 1853.

In 1840 the Ballyknock society met at 'Lyllys'. In those days, one's address was the townland in which one lived; this is vital in sorting out the various strands of the family, where the same Christian names are used in lateral strands.

On his death in 1889, Robert was buried in Magheragall parish churchyard (the Methodist Church did not have a graveyard). This information is from the *Belfast News Letter* as his name is not entered in the parish register. With the help of the Rector of Magheragall, Rev. G.A.Cheevers, we have located the grave but there is no headstone so we cannot say who else is buried there. The grave was registered in the name of Mary Agnes Lilley of 17 Penrose Street, Belfast. Mary Agnes was the youngest daughter, a half sister of Samuel. The street directory did not help with Mary Agnes, perhaps she was a lodger. Samuel's brothers and sisters have also been traced, as far as possible. The eldest, William, born 1837, died 1865, the day before his mother died. Robert, born 1839, married Jane Mullagh in Frederick Street Wesleyan Church in 1869 and emigrated to America; Henry married Mary Jane Whiteside from Bessbrook in 1871; Deborah and Joseph we were unable to trace; Sarah Jane married John McWatters the founder of the bakery of that name in Cromac Street, Belfast. They are buried in Knockbreda parish churchyard and their grandchildren are still alive and well in Belfast. The youngest, Elizabeth, was not followed through, nor were the two step sisters. Robert's will was granted probate 9 months after his death; his effects were valued at £174 12 0d. His son-in-law John McWatters was left all houses and land plus £150; his wife got £30; his two daughters by his second marriage received £20 each whereas the two from the first marriage received only £1 each. Samuel and Henry received £10 each and Joseph's children (presumably Joseph was dead) received £5 each. Robert's wife and children (again, Robert must have died) were to get five shillings each if they returned from America. Within a year there is no further trace of the family in Magheragall; it seems that John McWatters realised his capital to help found the bakery.

The age quoted on Robert's death certificate took us back to a birth date c. 1809. The church registers by this time had suggested that we look at other townlands, e.g. Ballykeel Artifinny, but more particularly Ballyknock, which is actually in the parish of Moira. Indeed in Ballyknock there was more than one Lilley family, but again the Downshire leasebook pointed out the one which we sought. On 1 January 1806 Robert Lilly took out a lease from the Marchioness of Downshire (the 3rd Marquis was still a minor) for a farm of 11 acres 2 roods and 11 perches in the townland of Ballyknock, together with the dwelling house thereon. He undertook to build within three years a good and substantial dwelling house of brick and stone and good lime mortar, 35 feet long, 15 feet wide inside, 2 stories, 15 feet high at the least; the stable was to be 25 feet in length, 20 feet in width with a loft, 15 feet high. The barn was to be 35 feet long, 15 feet wide and 15 feet high. All buildings were to be covered with good slate and the house was not to be built within 3 perches of the road or highway. The lease commenced on 1 November 1805, when Robert was aged 36. By checking later rentals, we know that he was alive in 1816, age 47 and 1827, age 58 but the lease expired on 24 January 1835. Clearly we were back another generation, this was Robert of Magheragall's father. At this point, a friend lent us a copy of Crookshanks' *History of Methodism in Ireland,* published in 1798 and a very rare volume. In Lisburn on 2 April 1798, 32 stewards signed a Commission separating the new 'Wesleyan' Methodists from the old Primitive Methodists i.e., they would no longer accept the sacraments of the Anglican church. The name Robert Lilly was one of these 32; 1 can now say that my wife's great great grandfather was one of the founders of the Methodist Church in Ireland.

If Robert was 36 in 1805, he was born c. 1769. We know that William's (of Taughblane) eldest son, Joseph was born c. 1744 (12 years old in 1756) and that his third son, William was born c.1748 (8 years old in 1756); it is almost certain that Robert was a younger son, if not the youngest, of William. By the time he grew up, there was no room for him on the family farm in Taughblane and he took out a lease on his own account of a farm in Ballyknock. It must also be remembered that John Wesley paid many visits to Ireland over these years and preached in Lisburn on several occasions; Robert was evidently impressed by the missionary zeal of the founder of Methodism. We do not have an exact date of death for this Robert, we will call him Robert (1), but we can assume it was in 1835, the date the lease expired. When the lease was taken out in 1805/6, it did not refer to any lives other than Robert's own. We do, however, have an entry in the Hillsborough parish register on 12 January 1844, for the burial of Elizabeth Lilly, widow, age 70, of Ballyknock. It seems certain that this was Robert's widow, but there was no entry for Robert when he was buried.

Robert (1)'s eldest son William married Alice Law and can also be traced in the Hillsborough registers; they inherited Ballyknock, but William died in 1845, by which time Robert (2) had moved on and the third son Joseph took over the family farm. (In fact, William and Alice's son Henry lived with his Uncle Joseph at Ballyknock.) Joseph was born in 1813 and married Mary Graham; they had two daughters, Maggie and Annie. Joseph died in 1897 and the surviving daughter, Annie, in 1909, when the Ballyknock property was sold and the house contents auctioned. (All this family can be checked in Hillsborough parish churchyard.)

A study of the Downshire estate maps helped to locate the Ballyknock property. It lay on the bank of the River Lagan and the house which Robert Lilly built is still in existence. Although somewhat enlarged, its frontage is still recognisable as the house specified in the Downshire lease. It is called Lany House and when I visited it with its recent owner, he was able to point out the flood banks on the river which had been built by Joseph Lilly; in fact, his neighbour recalled his parents being present at the auction of the contents of the house in 1909! Lany House was recently on the market at an asking price of over £1/4m.

Having established an unbroken generational line, we can now try to understand the house moves, or rather the farm moves of each generation. Robert (1) was brought up on the farm in Taughblane and when he realised that he would not inherit the farm, he moved out to Ballyknock, which was perhaps a mile distant but at a much lower level and still within the Downshire Kilwarlin estate. Perhaps the proximity of Moira, which was a prominent centre of the new Methodism, was an influence in this decision. Robert (2) had probably married Jane in 1833, as the circuit class lists them as together in that year living in Upper Maze, very close to Ballyknock and still within the Kilwarlin estate. An undated map of the Maze leases on the estate shows Robert Lilly as a tenant of one of a row of long narrow holdings not far from the race course; the same row of long narrow holdings is still there, albeit with modern bungalows. As soon as he was prosperous enough, he took out a lease of a farm of just over 6 acres at Cross Lane, Magheragall, from the Hertford estate on the Antrim side of the River Lagan and within a mile or so of the Maze. This appears to have been in the early 1850s. This farm was within a few hundred yards of the new railway line which had recently been extended beyond Lisburn, with a halt at Magheragall. (The site is now occupied by a concrete block works.) Rail travel was beginning to catch on and it probably seemed the right thing to do. This was the generation which was moving off the land and into the city in search of work and this is just what at least two of his sons did, Robert and Samuel. Robert appears to have got digs in the Sandy Row area (the address on his marriage certificate) and he was married in Frederick Street Wesleyan Methodist Church (whose registers are held by the Salem congregation at Rathcoole); Samuel was living at Peter's Hill and no doubt worshipped at Frederick Street, but was married at University Road. Samuel and Eliza's family were all baptised in Donegall Square Methodist Church.

The second part of this article will describe our efforts to go backwards from 1756, but before doing so, it would be appropriate to recount the solving of a small problem along the way. Kathleen was researching her father's work in the Belfast College of Art in the early years of this century; the problem arose from the fact, that a catalogue showed damask designs by one William Lilley, as well as her father Herbert. Who was William? Although Bertie's elder brother was William, he was known as Eddie and, although he was in the linen industry, he was on the managerial staff rather than on the design staff. The only thing to do was to approach the Belfast College of Technology (the former Municipal Technical Institute) to see if they had any old registers or lists of students. To our astonishment, they were able to produce a card index of each student who had ever attended the college, indeed a separate coloured card for each session attended, which gave name, age, address, courses taken and standard obtained! As well as Herbert at the College of Art, there was also a William Lilley with an address at McClure Street, Belfast. A trawl of the 1901 census on microfilm in PRONI revealed William, aged 11, one of five children of Richard and Agnes Lilley, respectively 40 and 38 years. They were Moravian, no doubt attending the little Moravian church in University Road nearby. We searched the indexes in Joyce House, Dublin for their marriage and when we got the certificate, found that Richard Lilley married Agnes Corbett on 18 March 1881 in the Primitive Methodist Church, Melbourne Street, Belfast *according to the usages of the Moravian Church.* By 'plotting' this information on our family tree, we were able to establish that this William was a great great grandson of Robert (1) and a great grandson of William, who had married Alice Law of Ballyknock; their son William had married a Sarah in the Moravian church in Kilwarlin and that line had remained members of the Moravian church. So Bertie and William were something like fifth cousins!

The customary modern spelling of the name was not always so; over the various sources consulted, many variants were found. The chief among these, particularly in the last century and which is still in use in some parts of the family, is Lillie. Other variants found included Lilly, Lily, Lylly and Luly but in our research we have taken them all to be the same name pronounced phonetically. A limited number of Christian names also tended to be repeated from generation to generation. As already stated, the first born in each family often received the name William; in the early generations Robert, Samuel and Joseph were almost the only names used, with Richard and Isaac being added later.

Having filled up many branches of the tree and the main direct line by now complete as far back as 1756, with a dotted line to 1722, the problem now was to go backwards; as most genealogists working in Irish sources know, to go beyond this date takes one into uncharted territory and, although one may find individuals with the right surname, to connect them with certainty into a relationship with those one has already pinpointed, would be quite remarkable. Time consuming though it was, we trawled the registers of Moira and Magheralin parish churches, Dromore Cathedral and Lisburn Cathedral; Magheralin and Lisburn have registers going back to the late seventeenth century. Three of these proved to be blank, but the registers for Lisburn produced a few more Lillys. There is a baptismal register from 1639-1645, but the second volume covers the period 1661-1720 for baptisms and burials and 1664-1739 for marriages. The information was insufficient, however, to connect them to Joseph, buried 1722/3 or William of 1756. For the record, the entries are:

Baptisms:

John Lilly	Lisburn 21.8.1686	son of John
Richard Lilly	Lisburn 25.6.1718	son of John
Ann Lilly	Lisburn 4.11.1718	daughter of Joseph
Esther Lilly	Lisburn 2.1.1726	daughter of Andrew

Marriages:

John Lilly & Elizabeth Holiday of Blaris	26.7.1681
John Lilliar & Margaret Taverner of Blaris	10.6.1690

Using these entries, one could tentatively insert possible relationships at the top of the tree. John & Elizabeth, married 1681 are probably the parents of John, born 1686, who in turn is probably the father of Richard, born 1718. Ann, born 1718 may have been the daughter of Joseph who died in 1723. At this period, we were fairly certain that there could only have been one Lilley family around the Lagan valley because of the paucity of names in the registers. These names in the Lisburn register suggest strongly that we are only one generation, or at the most two, from William of 1756. The point to be made, however, is that 1681 is positively the earliest date at which the name was recorded in the area. Although there are hundreds, if not thousands of baptisms and burials during the 1660s and 1670s, there are no other Lilleys to be found among them.

Where, then, did John and Joseph Lilly come from? Many years ago, the Dublin Parish Register Society published transcripts of several registers of seventeenth- and eighteenth-century Dublin parishes. Whilst a marriage as early as 1624 is recorded in St.John's, this is too far out to be counted. A Daniel Lilli was baptised in St.Michan's in 1666, but St.Catherine's yields the richest harvest of Lillys. Between 1680 and 1690, there are no fewer than 11 entries of the name, with the Christian names Abraham, James, John, William, Grace, Mary and Margaret. There are also 5 entries of the name in the published register of Derry Cathedral between 1691 and 1695,

James, John and Jeane. We might conclude that John Lilly arrived from Dublin, seeking work in the linen industry which was about to benefit from the arrival in Lisburn of the Huguenot colony under Crommelin. He came north, along with many others, married Elizabeth Holiday and settled down to work and raise a family.

The territory of Kilwarlin, in the Barony of Lower Iveagh, was held prior to the Restoration by Brian Rory Magennis, the townland of Taughblane being held under Magennis by Owen McKeenan. After the Restoration in 1660, the Kilwarlin estate was granted to Col.Arthur Hill, an ancestor of the Downshire dynasty, who would naturally have attracted protestant tenants with favourable leases to farms on the estate. Indeed what might loosely be called the upper Lagan valley along with the upper Bann valley was intensely populated during the four decades from 1660-1700. The parishes of Lisburn, Shankill (Lurgan), Seagoe (Portadown), Hillsborough, Dromore, Seapatrick (Banbridge) and Magheralin, alone with a number of smaller parishes, all built new churches during these 40 years to cater for the needs of the incoming people who followed the religion of the Established Church. It created, perhaps, the most intensely Anglican settlement at that time outside Dublin itself. A perusal of the surnames on the leases of the Kilwarlin estate reveals many English names such as Archer and Mercer, still represented to-day, a fact which points strongly to the origin of the incoming tenants.

Although it can only be, at the moment, a surmise that the Lilleys came from Dublin, it seems to us to be more correct that they came through Dublin, using it only as a staging post for entry into Ireland. Edward McLysaght, who has written numerous books on the origins of Irish surnames, writes:

> The sept of MacAilghile, formerly anglicised MacAlilly but now usually Lilly, Lilley or Lillie, is a branch of the MacGuires of Fermanagh, and its members today are mainly located in its original homeland around Enniskillen, though families of the name are found in other counties bordering on Fermanagh. Its origin is dealt with in several of the old genealogical works such as the Book of Ballymote and MacFirbis. The surname Lilley (akin to Lely) is well-known in England where it is indigenous; but, though, at least four appear in the army list of the Cromwellian and Restoration period,

very few of that stock settled in Ireland and it may be assumed that Irish Lilleys are MacAlillys, especially if their families belong to central Ulster.

Whilst we admit that, during our research, it was quite evident that there was another concentration of Lilleys around Fermanagh and Roscommon, who undoubtedly would have been related to the Maguires, it was equally evident that our Lilleys did not stem from that source. We had always felt that the name had a French ring about it and that the similarity to the city of Lille would be worth investigating. This was the part of France whence the Huguenots had come to Britain and many, the figure has been put at 10,000, came to Ireland. If our dating is correct, the Lilleys arrived in the Lisburn area shortly before the main arrival of Huguenots which was in the 1690s after the Revocation of the Edict of Nantes in 1685. Again, if our dating is correct, they arrived slightly before the arrival of the Williamite army, although, as that army was quartered in Lisburn, they may well have served in it.

Kathleen and I decided last summer to visit the Society of Genealogists in London in order to search for the name in the England of the period, or even perhaps in France. Whilst we were able to note Lillys all over the country, the most promising family, having all the right Christian names, was in Bradford, Yorkshire in the first half of the seventeenth century. Another family in Bromsgrove near Birmingham was documented from the father, William's, birth in 1468 until his death in 1532. But the indications pointed very strongly to France, particularly when we chanced on a reference to the name de l'Isle, which was often changed to Lilley in this country.

In the Society's extensive library, we found *The Registers oj the Protestant Church at Caen 1560-1572.* From 1564 onwards, we found many references to Robert Lilays, sometimes Lileys, who appeared to have an official function connected with baptism although he was not the minister performing the rite; it seemed that he presented the child for baptism. In the early years the residence was 'quartier de Vaucelles', but later they apparently moved to the 'quartier St.Etienne'. In 1568 a baptismal entry tells us that Robert's own son was baptised.

Cedit jour au prêche du matin fait au quartier de St. Jean par M Duval, a été baptisé le fils de Robert Lilays et de Jeanne, sa femme, au quartier de Vaucelles, laquel a été presenté par honorable homme Guillaume de Marne de quartier de St Jean, qui le nommé Pierre.

The Huguenot Society has published transcripts of the Registers of the various churches used by the French Protestant refugees in England (and also in Ireland). Here we found references to Isaac de Lillers and Jean de Lillers in the period 1643-1649. Guillaume Carbonel of Caen, merchant, married Elizabeth, daughter of Jean de Lillers in Threadneedle Church in the 1680s; they had seven sons. Closer to home, Charles Francois de l'Isle of Valenciennes served with the Duke of Schomberg, was pensioned in 1692 and was buried in St Patrick's Cathedral, Dublin on 7 October 1693.

The work is ongoing and we hope to follow up some of the French lines of enquiry in due course. To summarise, therefore, the work so far, it is almost certain that the family arrived in the Lagan valley not earlier than 1680, but whether they came directly from England or through Dublin is not proved. It is also fairly certain that the family is French in origin and of Protestant extraction, leaving France during the period of the persecution of Protestants.

A memorial to the artistic and design capabilities of Herbert R Lilley exists in a collection of embroidered textiles donated by him in February 1967 to the Ulster Folk and Transport Musuem and known as 'The Lilley Collection'. It is among groups of specimens referred to in *Textile Collections of the World*, where it is described as being 'of embroidered handkerchiefs'.

Joseph bur. Blaris 1722/3

William (Taughblane) 1756

Joseph George William Samuel Robert=Elizabeth
1769/1835 | 1774/1844

Marriah Addison=Alicia

William=Alice Robert=(1) Jane (2) Eliza Nelson Joseph=Mary Graham Samuel James=Mary Malcolm
1793/1845 1809/1889 1813/1897 /1892

(2) Margaret Mary Agnes
1869/? 1874/?

William Robert Henry Deborah Joseph Samuel Sarah Jane Elizabeth
1837/186 1839/? 1841/? 1843/? 1844/? 1850/1898 1852/192 3 1855/?

Eliza Jane Wilson
c.1861/1922
=

Herbert Robert Mabel Winifred Walter Ernest Charles George Gertrude Florence
1886/1970

William Edwin Campbell

Margaret Marion Stuart
1898/1982

Kathleen=J. Fred Frankin Brian=Jennifer Brooke
1928/ 1931/

M Gillian=Nicholas Wells Susan K. J F Neal=Ingrid Boyd Simon J A=Clare Willis
1953/ 1954/ 1958/ 1962/

Honor Stuart Charity Conor
1990/ 1992/ 1994/ 1995/

Lucy Simon
1982/ 1984/

AMY CARMICHAEL OF DOHNAVUR (1867-1951)

by George Ruddock

When Amy Carmichael arrived in India in November 1895, nobody could have anticipated one of the most distinguished careers in recent Irish missionary endeavour. She had already spent a year in Japan and part of another year in Sri Lanka and had been recommended to the hills of South India for health reasons. Miss Carmichael never left India again, spent 54 years on the plains and lived in the village of Dohnavur from the end of 1901 till her death on 18 December 1951. In Dohnavur, she gathered her Family of children, especially girls who would otherwise have been dedicated to Temple service, with its honoured place in Hindu worship and a life of pampered prostitution.

Amy Carmichael was born in Millisle on 16 December 1867, the eldest child of prosperous Presbyterian flour millers. The family moved to College Gardens, Belfast about 1882, but the business began to fail and then her father died suddenly in 1885. In 1888, Amy and her mother were recommended to separate situations in England. Amy Carmichael made her personal commitment to Christian faith as a teenager – and active work followed almost immediately. Henry Montgomery, then superintendent of the Belfast City Mission, often took his own daughter and Amy with him on his rounds. It was clear that the church was making little impact on the factory girls, the 'shawlies'. To begin with, Amy persuaded her own minister, Dr Park of Rosemary Street, to let her run a class for 'her girls' in the Church Hall on Sunday mornings. That in itself was more than unconventional – because 'shawlies' did not wear hats to church!

Success carried the work into every day except Saturday, under the auspices of the YWCA – and into its own building, called, tellingly, 'The Welcome', rather than the Welcome Hall. In her work with the mill girls, Miss Carmichael fixed on three principles to which she held ever afterwards.

– Find out everything possible about the conditions in which the 'shawlies' lived and worked. She badgered her brother, an apprentice engineer in the Northern Counties Railway shops, to tell her 'just what kind of conversation they would hear' – and was both sadder and wiser, given a feisty sample of workshop gossip.

– No appeal for money. 'It was enough,' she wrote, telling the story years later, 'to ask God only for money for His work.'[1] An iron hall to seat 500 could be erected for £500. The money came as a single donation from one benefactor, in memory of a friend who had died.

– Spiritual welfare was the first priority – and that determined recruitment of helpers. The girls were offered classes in sewing and in general education. They were given meals. But cooks and instructors must not just be good in their own field and willing to help. They must first and foremost be committed to the Christian outreach of 'The Welcome'.[2]

In England, Amy forged close links with the family of Robert Wilson, an elderly Friend from Cumberland. He introduced her to Quaker worship, involved her in his work with the local Baptist Sunday School and took her to the Anglican parish church for evensong. Robert Wilson was also one of the early leaders of the Keswick Convention, for whom he chose the motto text 'All One in Christ Jesus'.[3] When Miss Carmichael set out for India, it was as a 'Keswick' missionary, to work with the Church of England Women's Mission. It was a measure of broadmindedness on all sides that the CMS leaders and an Irish Presbyterian agreed to work together, although Miss Carmichael made it clear she would not ask for financial support. The fourth principle of Miss Carmichael's work lay in her broad sympathy with Christians of differing traditions.

South India has a large Christian church – so numerous that friends of missions in the British Isles might consider the Tinnevelly district, where Miss Carmichael soon settled, almost as Christian as a district at home including the problems of nominal membership and limited understanding of the Christian faith. The deep difference was that South Indian society remained profoundly Hindu in structure, customs and morality. (There were also Moslem localities.) Tinnevelly district was an orthodox stronghold where the Brahmin establishment held undisputed sway, vigorously asserted against threat or slight. In decades when the Christian church grew most rapidly, converts abandoned caste and thus brought risk of defilement to the community and to the religious rituals that Hindus prize so highly, persecution was vigorous and ostracism widespread. In any case, Christian work in South India found its warmest welcome not at all in every strata of society, but among two Hindu sub-castes. Dohnavur had been built as a village of refuge for persecuted Christians. A German Count Dohna paid for the church. (Dohnavur means Dohna's village.)

In December 1896, Miss Carmichael went to Tinnevelly District[4] at the invitation of a couple who had worked there with the Church Missionary Society since 1884. The Reverend Thomas Walker offered to teach Amy the Tamil language and hoped to employ her skills in church work and evangelism. It was agreed that she should live as a member of the Walker household. By 1898, she had formed a Women's Band for itinerant work. The Indians dubbed them the 'Starry Cluster' and the name stuck. They met with some success and much opposition.[5]

Amy Carmichael was unconventional by any standards. Her levels of Christian devotion set her apart even among missionaries. A former member years afterwards did a skit on how Amy raced ahead of the Starry Cluster and kept looking at her watch to make sure no time was wasted. The locals watched Amy's speed and called her the 'Hare'. They were also concerned that she had a fatal attraction for children. Right from the start, Amy wanted to work with Indians as colleagues. Once in Tinnevelly, she adopted Indian dress, not then widely approved among Europeans. Indians who knew her well admired Amy's taste in saris. She was amused to find that her visits in the villages gave rise to discussion. Only a man wore the solar topi. Only a widow neglected to oil her hair. Miss Carmichael found other reasons to be concerned. When the first two girl converts came, separately, they were just old enough to decide for themselves – and resisted all family pressures and blandishments to go back home and keep the family faith. They were therefore homeless. The missionaries had obvious responsibilities to them. Amy added them to her household – and took them with her on holiday with her to very British Ooty.[6] Miss Carmichael was shocked when children who showed some interest in her preaching were consigned to long and severe hardship.

Some were sent to distant relatives, or otherwise disappeared. There was a considerable body of evidence that enquirers of any age might be given drugs or even poison to save them from association with foreigners and Christians.

On 6 March, 1901, the Walkers, Miss Carmichael and the Women's Band returned to the mission bungalow in a town they had not visited in almost a year. At 6.30 a.m. next morning, a Christian woman from the town arrived with a seven year old girl. Her name, said the child, was Preena. (The name translates as Pearl eyes.) She had escaped from the Temple in the next village, to which her mother gave her soon after her father died. The child had already absconded once before. Homesick and disliking the Temple training, she had walked twenty miles home to her mother.

The Temple women had followed. They reminded the mother that her late husband had been a leading Hindu scholar and warned that the gods would be angry if the girl was not given back to them, so her mother compelled her to return. The Temple Women branded her hands to ensure that she would not defy them again. They also tried to frighten her by talk of the 'child-catching Missie Hare...'. But then the child heard the Women talking about her and saying she must soon be 'tied to the god'. So this time, she had ran to Miss Carmichael (Missie Hare) and insisted that she wanted to stay. Late the previous evening, the Christian woman found her in the street and took her home because it was late. They set out early to go back to the Temple, but the girl refused to go. Nobody had known the Band was in the bungalow. The Temple Women soon appeared to claim the fugitive. Miss Carmichael asked them who they were. They said, straightforwardly, 'Servants of the Gods' and that the girls mother had given her to them. But, for all the fuss and threats, they produced no evidence that the girl was theirs. So she became part of the mission household. Preena talked about her life and training in the Temple and 'told us things that darkened the sunlight'.[6]

Everybody who watched a Hindu festival had seen beautiful, richly dressed girls up on the Car beside the God. It was quite a different matter to find out how the girls were recruited and trained and what their life was like. Miss Carmichael went after information like a sleuth, talking to Indians, enquiring from the government, writing to missionaries. No Hindu would talk to a foreigner, save in vague generalities, about this old practice dying out with the old Temple Women, given government pressure and modern education. Most missionaries knew little. Temple life went on behind doors closed to them. Some wrote to ask if Amy might be exaggerating the problem. Government Collectors had more contacts and insight, but no proof. One missionary sent a pamphlet he had written on the problem twenty years earlier, with the sad comment 'Result – Nil'.

Miss Carmichael continued to travel and preach. Often, with a colleague from the Starry Cluster, she stayed in accommodation for poor travellers. Amy was sometimes taken for a Brahmin widow, sometimes ignored in the bustle. They talked to everybody, including garland makers who supplied the Temple. In May 1905, she met Mr F. R. Hemingway of the Indian Civil Service, who stressed the need for careful notes and details of individual cases.[7] She issued the careful *caveat* that 'India is a land where generalisations are deceptive. So we have kept to the South – to the areas where the evil is distinctly and recognisably religious.'[8]

It was finally established that a Temple Child would be:

– always of high Caste in order to be a 'Servant of the God',
– a fatherless girl of good birth, especially one born after the father's death whom the family will not adopt: the widow will earn merit through the dedication and the child will never be a widow;
– an orphan left with grandparents;
– a child of a mixed marriage – which are not common occurrences, but they often produced Temple children or boy actors and musicians;
– a dedication to avert disaster (as illness) for the family: sometimes, a family gave a girl in each generation;
– a child widow, if very young;
– an illegitimate child, sometimes children of widows misused, often by in-laws, and then forced to get rid of the child;
– a very beautiful child, kidnapped.

Money was often paid for suitable children, from 2½ rupees and a cloth to 100 rupees and the promise of a field. There was also a traffic in suitable girls from parts of the country where Temple women were unknown.

The life of the Temple Children also became clearer with enquiry. They might be trained in Temple houses, in mixed houses, which give dance training, or in village houses which 'train girls for the use of those whose caste forbids them to go to a Hindu temple'. Most of the children went to school to learn reading, some to mission school. They learned dancing and had their limbs massaged to aid subtle movement. They learned stories from an 'elder brother'. Many children described the stories and poems as 'unclean', but they were forced to listen, familiarity made distaste less sharp and 'instinct is perverted, bewildered, deceived., incapable of choice'.[9] Finally, the child was 'married to the god'. That is what Preena feared, for the idiom is 'tied to the god'. If the wedding must be kept secret, the gold wedding symbol – 'tali' – was placed round the neck under a garland of flowers and the priest touched it. If the celebration could safely be public, there was a wedding procession, with another girl dressed as the bridegroom. Marriage to the god conferred great honour – and the girls were taught that. The ceremony was performed very young, at the age of eight or nine. One girl near Dohnavur, married at the age of five, 'knew only the rejoicing and pleasure'.[10] No other marriage was possible, once a girl was married to the god.

It was unlucky to see a widow first thing in the morning, but high good luck to see a Servant of the god. They were safe alone in crowds. The proverbial description said 'an honoured name is theirs, which no virtuous woman would bear.' Servants of the gods were honoured and they were despised. There Amy Carmichael instanced the English-educated son of a Rajah who used vile proverbs to dismiss a Servant, but whose wife was attended at the name-giving ceremony by a Servant who presented his son to the priest. And, towards the end, she wrote:

> And I have seen the scorn and the shock of awakening to its existence is sometimes very visible on the child or girl whose life up to that time has been happy enough. I have seen such a child cry her heart out under the first hard word which told her what she had never known before crushed to the dust as the world tramples over her. The sense of this double treatment being unjust never seems to trouble the Hindu ... but I have known Hindus better than their creed.

Mr Walker had to teach a group of divinity students through the early months of 1902, so they went to Dohnavur, where the compound was large enough to accommodate everybody. It was a secluded place, a couple of miles off anything like a road and more than twenty miles from the railway. Isolation afforded more shelter for children rescued from Temple service. The locality was free from malaria. The mountains to the west of the village Amy described as 'strong, tranquil and serene'. And they found that the compound was built on a subartesian basin, a great help as the family grew. Three girls in need had been given into Amy's care in June 1901, but no more Temple children were rescued for three years. June 1904 saw seventeen children in Dohnavur, including six definitely saved from Temple service.

One father agreed to give Amy his eight-year-old daughter, rather than sell her to a Temple woman – if he was paid one hundred rupees. The deal was done reluctantly as the only way to save the girl and does not seem to have set the feared precedent. Among the six were the first Temple babies. An Indian pastor, watching Temple women with children, persuaded them to give him the baby, thirteen days old. Another baby arrived from another pastor. A third baby came. The work seemed on its way at last. Within twelve months, all three babies were dead. It was a pattern often repeated, that babies arrived who would not thrive. Sometimes, they may have been given away for that reason. These three – and others later – were born after the father's death when the mother was distracted with grief and under severe widow's penance. Some babies do not thrive on artificial food and it was then impossible to persuade any of the local women to act as wet nurses – even for a baby taken to church on Christmas Eve 1904! ('It is not our custom'). There were later occasions when there were hesitations about taking a sickly baby, but then 'we have discouraged those who are willing to help us and the next baby in danger is taken straight to the house where its welcome was assured'.[11]

By the time she wrote *Lotus Buds*[12] in 1909, Miss Carmichael had a more general understanding of the situation concerning Temple women. She acknowledged that the British government must maintain its policy of religious neutrality, although she was distressed by the fact that the Penal Law – which forbade both sale of children and child marriage (below the age of 16) – was so little help. A sale could seldom be proved and the intention to marry never presumed, even from the distinctive training. 'Imagine', lamented Miss Carmichael, 'watching a Bluebeard whet a butcher's knife, especially if he was known to have a cupboard full of pendant heads'. Part of the problem, of course, was that public opinion opposed Bluebeards, whereas 'service to the gods' had strong, age-old religious sanction. There were social reformers in Bombay and Madras among the educated classes, but even they could not rally public opinion behind reform. More than one Christian judge was consulted and given detailed case histories. The answer was always the same. All evidence would be disputed. Even if an intention to offend could be proved, the child would simply be returned to her parents and then to the Temple. When cases concerning 'marriage to the gods' occasionally.reached court, the practice was treated as 'customary'. Miss Carmichael was glad to establish and state that Temple prostitution was a parasite on pure Hinduism, forbidden in the Vedas and unknown until the third century A.D.[12] The rise of the Caste seems to date from ninth and tenth centuries. The 1901 Census found that they constitute a regular Caste having 'its own customs ... and councils ... and hold a position which is without parallel in any other country'. The closely allied Caste of Hindu musicians are 'now practically the sole repository of Indian music, the system of which is probably one of the oldest in the world'. *Lotus Buds* saluted the efforts of some Indian States to end Temple service and quoted newspaper calls and reports of the resolutions of Hindu Social Reformers in the *Indian Times*, the *Epiphany* and most extensively from the *Madras Mail*. The *Madras Mail* of 2 January 1909 reported reform in Mysore State. Hastening slowly like every civil service, they began in 1892 by defining legitimate Temple services, decreed in 1899 that women paid on the major Temple establishments would no longer be permitted to dance and that their allowances would cease on the death of the current holders. The caste tried to fight back, but after almost fifteen years when the public had grown accustomed to the absence of Temple women from some important Temples, the government held its ground.

It also stated that

'Shastraic authorities (show) that... singing and dancing in the presence of the deity are also prescribed.... It is however observed that in the case of Temple women, personal purity and rectitude of character and a vow of celibacy were consider essential'!

Finally, the government hoped that this good example would bear fruit 'where the Temple woman evil is more notorious than ... in Mysore'. Miss Carmichael commented, for her English readers, 'the high-minded Hindu – and there are such, let it not be forgotten – revolts from the degradation and pollution of this travesty of religion and will abolish it where he can'.

It was as a result of her work that enquiries were made by the Secretary of State for India in London to the Government of India regarding the dedication of children to Hindu gods. In a footnote to the second edition of *Lotus Buds* in 1912, there is the following comment on reform. 'Irrespective of nationality or religion, whoever has worked for and won the deliverance of the child should be allowed to act as guardian.' That would have solved one of the greatest hindrances to Dohnavur's work.

There were seventeen children at Dohnavur between the spring and summer of 1906. By 1907, adults and children together numbered seventy and by 1913, one hundred and forty. There was steady and continuous growth thereafter.[13] For all that, the work was not without its losses, hardships and hindrances. December 1906 saw an outbreak of cholera in Dohnavur village, which did not cross the gates of the compound, even with those who went in and out with such medical support as they could offer.

It was a constant concern that none of the Dohnavur workers had any medical training. The best immediate suggestion in September 1905 was to open a nursery beside the nearest hospital, a day and a half from Dohnavur by bullock cart. The most senior Indian worker took charge, with three nurses and five trainees. In the summer of 1907, the nurseries were very full. There was an outbreak of dysentry; seventeen of the children sickened and ten died. Occasionally, parents changed their minds about giving their daughters to Dohnavur and reclaimed them; sometimes, other members of a family made trouble

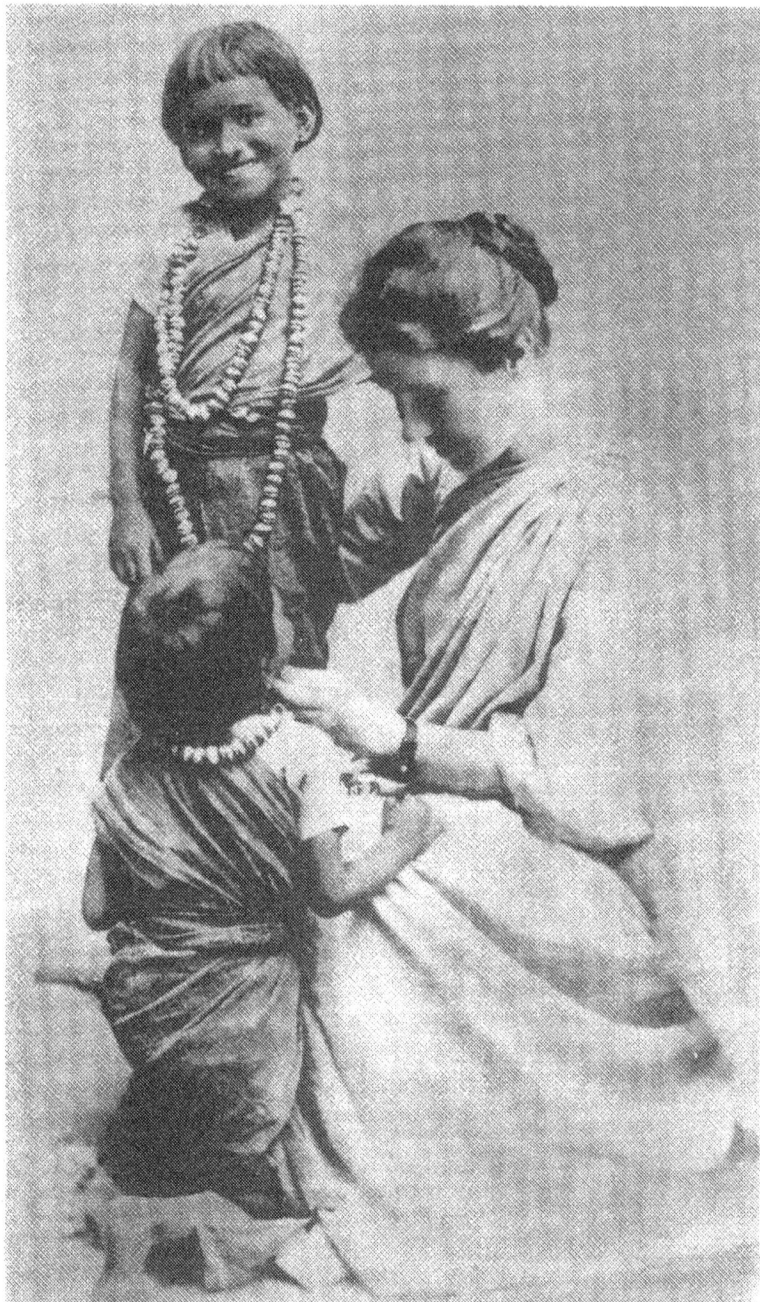

Amy Carmichael, known as 'Amma', with 2 Temple children

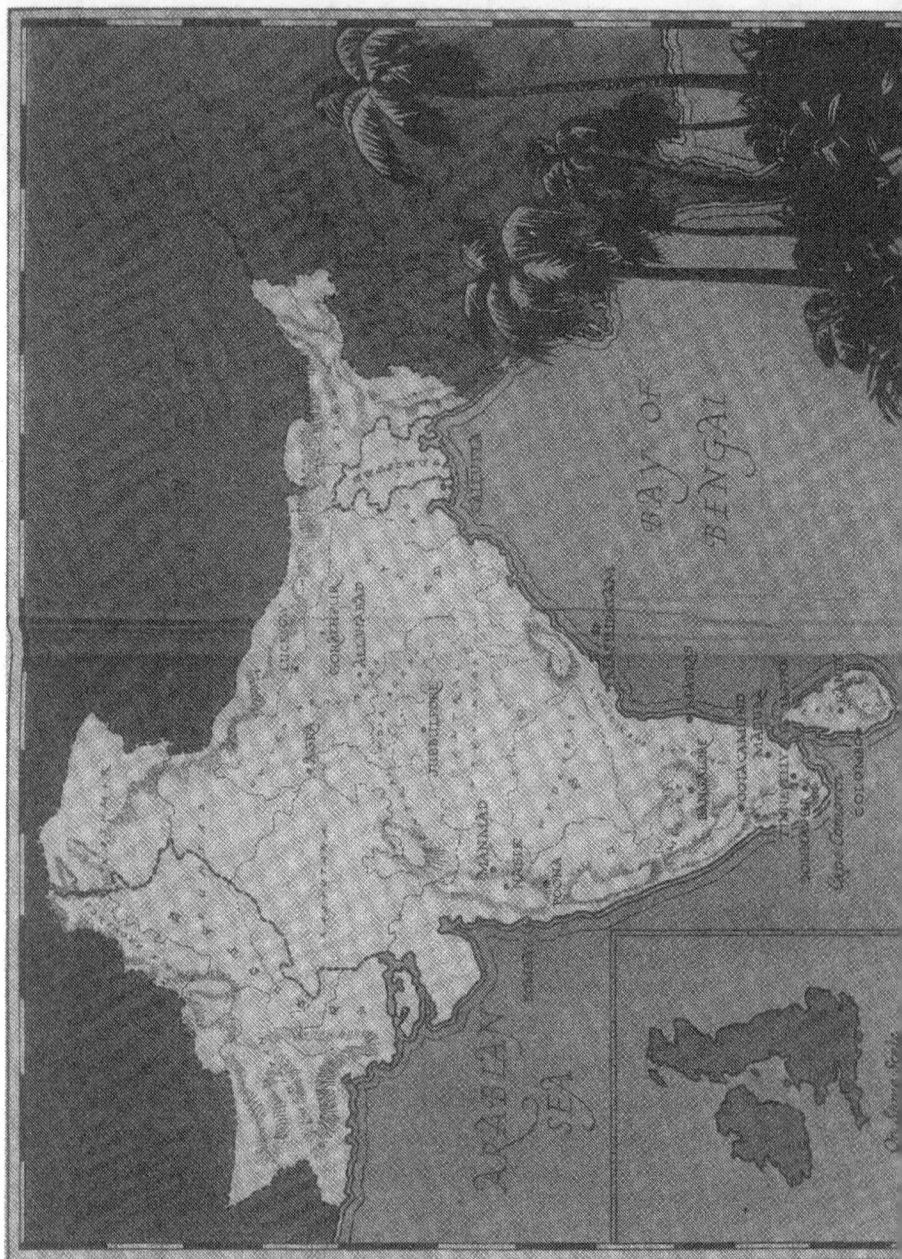

Map showing location of Tinnevelly in southern India, where Amy Carmichael was based.

- and, though few were pressed,there were countless threats of litigation. One case – of an orphan girl who inherited land – dragged on from March 1909 till April 1911.

The last three weeks of August 1912 were dreadful. The lady in Ooty died suddenly, who had kept open house for all Miss Carmichael's company, Indian and European alike. Then one of the most attractive five year olds died suddenly. Four days later, the Reverend Thomas Walker died without warning, while away on a preaching tour. His leadership and advice had been key to the developing work and it was fitting in Indian eyes that it should be led by a man. As Miss Carmichael wrote in wistful understatement, he 'would have been such a stay through the years of War'.[14] And another girl of eight died within a week of Mr Walker. 1913 brought an unusual epidemic of malaria, with seventy children sick, although none died. And so it went on.

Provision of workers and of buildings commonly came after the need for them, or since nobody knew how many children would be rescued. No prior limits were set, except to pass some arrivals on to other missions, as the number of Temple children increased. The first nurseries were built towards the end of 1906, on a field adjoining the compound...

> ...of sun-dried bricks, with earthen floor and thatched roofs, but too much time had to be spent in keeping the termites out of the walls ... and thatched roofs were unsafe, for conversion ... from among the caste people may (deliver) a lighted rag on the thatched roof of the offender; so, when the money came to enable us to do it, we used burnt brick and tiles.[15]

By 1912, there were nine nurseries. After that, building was almost part of the routine. In 1917, land was bought in the 'grey forest' at three thousand feet in the mountains nearby and a hot weather retreat was built for use twice a year. A Syrian Christian helped to secure land to the south, where 'Pavilions'[16] was built for children less robust or less able academically; and a small house called Joppa[17] was built by the sea at Cape Cormorin, as a retreat for tired Dohnavur workers. As the family grew, the village church could not accommodate them along with the regular congregation, so a separate House of Prayer was opened in 1927. (An architect and a builder wrote inviting themselves to stay over Christmas 1925.) The final major project was a hospital, begun in 1929. The biggest single expansion,[18] in the work among children came unannounced, on 14 January 1918. A bullock cart jingled up to the bungalow in the late evening and a tired woman handed over a bundle. There was nothing very unusual about that – but this baby was a boy!

Miss Carmichael had long been concerned that boys trained to perform music and drama were little better off than girls trained for the Temple. In November 1919, Amy and an Indian companion got in at last to a house where boys were trained for the drama. They bought tickets and asked the seller casually where the boys were living. He told them – and the boys welcomed them in, until the manager discovered the guests twenty minutes later. Then they attended the show. It had affinities with Shakespeare's theatre. All the actors were boys and both script and performance were heavily inclined to the bawdy.

The number of boys at Dohnavur increased slowly but steadily. There were seventy or eighty in 1926.[19] Separate buildings were needed at once. Indian custom would not allow boys and girls to be brought up together, or even to share the same classrooms. And workers were needed too.

The first nurse came in 1907 and a doctor soon after, but her health broke down and it was 1924 before a doctor came to stay. The first worker to come in response to Miss Carmichael's writing, arrived in 1910 to do 'whatever helps most' – as was asked of all. Teachers were much needed. One came to run a kindergarten, but her health broke down too. When Mr Walker died in 1912, two sisters, old India hands, felt they should offer at least temporary assistance – and one of them was in charge of all the education at Dohnavur for years to come. *A Time to Die* records doubts expressed about the old-fashioned teaching methods – but they seemed to work, even if she had not done the circular tours of curriculum development. The first man from overseas came in 1922, but he was a builder and farmer. It was not till 1926 that a permanent leader was found for the boys' work. Indian workers were as welcome as expatriates, so long as they met the high standards of Christian dedication and were willing for straightforward, unremitting hard work with none of the gaps allowed, say, in an appointment to school work: Dohnavur was the children's home. Miss Carmichael always described it as the 'missionary scrap heap' (!) – an isolated and unavoidably cloistered environment beset by heat and disease. India in general deputes the care of small children to servants and does not much esteem primary teaching, so that Indian workers were unlikely to come to Dohnavur under any illusions, especially since nobody was paid a salary. It was possible, overseas, to see the place in a rosy light which faded rather, when put to live with small boys, teach handcrafts and train a choir. Some workers stayed only a short time, although a number moved to other appointments in India. The first nurse was not the only arrival to wonder 'Have I been here for only one day?' and not a few never left again.

The Dohnavur Fellowship was legally established as an independent body in 1927, ending the loose association with the Church of England Women's Mission, much diluted as workers joined from a variety of countries and backgrounds. The CMS happily handed over its property on the compound. The Fellowship set out its object 'to save children in moral danger; to train them to serve others; to succour the suffering...'. Most untypically among mission bodies at that time, there was no controlling body elsewhere, although the Fellowship has representatives in Britain and in other countries. And no appeal for money was made or authorised.

Most workers from overseas had private means or support of friends sufficient for their personal expenses and many Indian colleagues were similarly provided for. Outside friends were needed to rescue, feed and clothe, house and educate the children. One of the earliest books, *The Beginning of a Story*, said exactly that – and Miss Carmichael withdrew it from circulation because it came too close to tugging at the reader's pocket. The family and its supporters were asked to.pray for its finance, as for all else. It was simply reported each year that all needs had been met. Offers to sponsor individual children were redirected elsewhere, no child being certain to succeed, but money for specific purposes was welcome. It is.still fixed policy for the Dohnavur Fellowship to pay all bills on the day they are presented and never to go into debt.

Amy Carmichael's greatest achievement was the realisation of Dohnavur as a FAMILY. That was how she always referred to children and adults alike. Right from 1901, Miss Carmichael was called AMMA – mother in Tamil. European women were addressed as Sittie (mother's younger sister or aunt) Indian women as Accal (older sister) and all men as Annachie (older brother). There is a very strong sense of family in India and people identify with their birthplace. Children rescued from Temple service were cut off from their natural families, but were received into a new family at Dohnavur, which they identify as home for the rest of their lives. Indian parents are responsible for upbringing and education, but then, much more than in the west, for finding employment and for arranging marriages. Dohnavur filled all those roles. Many of the children found husbands or wives from outside Dohnavur, others inside it. Many went to outside jobs. But new children engaged the talents of some older girls from the beginning and an increasing number as the family grew. Miss Carmichael saw the hospital as a Christian contribution to the medical needs of the community, but also as a training ground for some of her children – and so it has proved. Dohnavur kept to the best of Indian style in building, dress, manners and hospitality. No beef is ever served. At bedtime, babies were 'annointed with oil, according to the custom of the East' and each had a personal sleeping mat, as in the best families.

Visitors to Dohnavur report on it unanimously as a happy and colourful place. It is impossible to read any of her books without recognising that Amy Carmichael was not just concerned for the children or perceptive about them. She enjoyed them enormously. That surprised her too. Before 1901, she had little to do with small babies. Amy's mother came for a long visit which included all of 1905 and was amazed at her success even with infants upset and unwell and in the middle of the night. She was not alone in remarking how little food or rest Amy got.

The infant nursery was dubbed the menagerie and the 'middle aged' babies, from two to four, were in the parrot house. Babies who arrived unnamed were called after flowers or jewels. (Some visitors were shocked to find that the children had English nicknames, often used in books and letters, like Froglet and Cheshire Cat – and Spider, because in Tamil, the name Chrysanthemum is one letter off Spider.)

There was the inevitable collection of questions – 'Are rocks young mountains?'– which provided one of the leads for the home-made schooling of the early years.

> We never suggested questions and never answered questions they did not ask. But we ran to meet their minds in welcome. It was a jolly kind of schooling and left many gaps but it had some uses.

Miss Carmichael loved flowers and grew them in profusion. She loved birds almost as much. Nature study was a core subject too. She sent for microscopes from England, because she had enjoyed one so much as a child. There was a great deal of laughter and singing. Amy had a gift for rhyming and could make up instant nonsense verse. She had learned to swim in Millisle and insisted that the children do the same on holiday in the forest. She loved celebration as much as the children. It was hard to be sure of birthdays, so the day of a child's arrival in Dohnavur was celebrated as 'Coming Day' and when numbers made individual parties impractical, there was a feast for all the children whose 'Coming Days' fell in the same week. Children deserve to be happy, she said. Often, she found that preoccupation with problems present or future was eased by the steady routine of work. She held final authority in matters of discipline and dealt strictly with miscreants and the children held her in some awe. There was a rule in the dormitories that children who felt they must cry should do so quietly. But her door was always open to the children and messengers could choose a toy to keep till bedtime. Amy set herself at least to see each child every day. She had a tricycle to help her get round the compound and the children liked to help it along. The church services kept the children in mind. There were responses to prayers. Temple towns were mentioned with the request: 'God save the children there.' There were brief silences borrowed from the Quakers. There were Indian instruments and a place for movement. New arrivals were brought to the front for all to see. Children too young to sing words were given flags to wave. Services were short – by conscious decision of one brought up among Victorian Presbyterians.

If visitors were impressed with Dohnavur, the family knew that harmony could be hard work. When people talked or wrote about the spiritual tone of their life, they would pray 'God make us what we seem to be'. Perfection among babies would make them anxious, but was 'a fear not pressing at present'. The work was never without its critics. If it was quickly conceded that the problem of Temple children did exist, there were always those who felt that the work would be easier if Miss Carmichael lowered the very high standards she demanded of staff and paid at least the Indian workers. She was astonished to be asked by an elderly guest to forgive an offence she had never heard of. He had been convenor of the commiittee that wanted her out of India when they read *Things As They Are*.

The greatest shock came at the beginning of 1919, when the Governor of Madras wrote to congratulate Miss Carmichael on her inclusion in the Royal Birthday Honours List, where she was awarded the Kaiser-i-Hind medal for services to the people of India. Horror is the only word for her reaction. She wrote asking leave to refuse. Friends finally persuaded her to accept the honour, but nothing could get her to the presentation ceremony. Nobody doubted that the award was well deserved. If nothing else, it was as clear a mark of support for her as the government could make.

Much of Miss Carmichael's influence outside Dohnavur came from her writing. It was natural that there should be letters about her work. Books were a more considerable achievement in the midst of such a busy schedule. Miss Carmichael wrote about the children and described work further afield. There were two missionary biographies and the stories of four Indian fellow workers. A visitor to Dohnavur persuaded her to tell how money came in and she did so in long retrospect. There were books of poems, some set to music and used in worship.

It was in devotional references that Miss Carmichael revealed her wide reading and sympathies. Her belief and teaching were firmly Protestant and her work draws from scripture and the commentaries of Puritans old and new. But she also found much encouragement in Thomas a Kempis' *Imitation of Christ*, the work of Brother Lawrence, the meditations of Julian of Norwich. She recognised that they had searched, as she did, for the excellence of the knowledge of Christ and knew what she called the 'joy of sacrificial living'. In the *Spiritual Letters of Pere Didon* she found a call like her own. 'I do not want people who come to me with certain reservations. In battle, you need soldiers who fear nothing.' It would misrepresent Amy Carmichael to see her as ecumenical in the current sense, but she might well claim the Irish Presbyterian ideal that Christians should not 'refuse light from any quarter'.

Thomas a Kempis makes reference to Gerhardt Groot and the Brothers of the Common Life that he founded about 1380. It was a lay order, with no vows. The members had regular daily employment, but willingly shared their resources and gave themselves to the free and happy service of God. In 1916, Miss Amy Carmichael invited seven of the Indian women to join her in similar vows of 'unreserved devotion, a life without fences'. They called themselves the Sisters of the Common Life. The Sisters met on Saturday mornings and studied the scriptures and the wide range of writers from whom Amy Carmichael drew inspiration. There was no necessary task that they would refuse or delay and they made no distinction between tasks sacred – and more laudable? – and secular. The group increased in size and there are still Sisters today, although no equivalent men's group was ever formed.

In September 1931, Miss Carmichael had a serious fall and never walked freely again. To the many prayers for healing the answer was 'No'. She turned increasingly to writing, much of it for the Family and not for publication, although posthumous selections were made. Many books were sent to Miss Carmichael too. Those on sickness she found of little help, since the writers were in full health and vigour. So began books like *Rose from Brier* and *Gold by Moonlight*, Christian reflections of patient to patient and on the sufferings of Christ.

She lived long enough to see her life's work reach fulfilment. One of the first laws passed after Indian independence by the Madras State Legislature made it an offence to dedicate children to Temple service. The lady member who introduced the bill said Miss Carmichael's writings had made her ashamed to be a Hindu. In 1948, the Indian Parliament made the practice illegal in all India.

APPENDIX 1
LIST OF AMY CARMICHAEL'S PUBLISHED WORKS

From Sunrise Land	1895
From the Fight	c.1901
Raisins	1901
Things as They Are	1901
Overweights of Joy	1903
Beginning of a Story	1906
Lotus Buds	1908
Continuation of a Story	1909
Walker of Tinnevelly	1914
Made in the Pans	1916
Ponnammal	1917
From the Forest	1918
Dohnavur Songs	1920
Nor Script	1921
Ragland	1922
Tables in the Wildnerness	1923
The Valley of Vision	1924
Minosa	1924
Raj (MS finished in 1924)	end 1926
The Widow of the Jewels	1928
Meal in a Barrel	1929
Gold Cord	1932
Rose From Brier	1932
Ploughed Under	1933
Gold by Moonlight	1934
Toward Jerusalem	1935
Windows	1936
If	1937
Figures of the True	1938
Pools and, the Valley of Vision	1938
Kohila	1938
His Thoughts Said...His Father Said	1939
Though the Mountains Shake	1941
Before the Door Shuts	1943
This One Thing	1948
Edges of His Ways	1950

Thou Guest...They Gather	1958
Wings (with music)	In the Press
Candles in the Dark	1981
Whispers of His Power	1982

NOTES

1. Bishop Frank Houghton: *Amy Carmichael of Donavur*, p.25. The (reluctantly) authorised biography and best single source.
2. 'The Welcome' survived long after the Carmichael family left Belfast
3. *Galatians* chapter 3, verse 28.
4. In 1900, Tinnevelly District was twice the size of Wales and twice as populous.
5. A missionary society asked Miss Carmichael to write about her evangelistic work, but returned the account, asking her to make it more optimistic. She filed it away. Friends visiting from England found it. Photographs were added and they saw it into print under the title *Things As They Are*.
6. Ootacamund, the very British summer capital of Madras State.
7. Much of this section follows Miss Carmichael's Typescript on *Temple Women and Children*, now among the Carmichael Papers in the Public Record Office of N. Ireland, Belfast. The early work at Dohnavur is described in greater detail in *Lotus Buds* for which the typescript clearly formed a basis.
8. *Lotus Buds* chapter 27.
12. Willoughby Legh, a friend from the Indian Civil Service advised on the writing of *Lotus Buds*, to put the stories about the children in Dohnavur first 'then people will be drawn on' to evidence about the Temple traffic.
13. *Gold Cord.*
14. *Gold Cord* p.95.
15. *Gold Cord* (*The Story of a Fellowship*) traces the work until 1931.
16. Three local kings used to meet there, in Royal Pavilions.
17. Peter's vision in *Acts* chapter 10 came to him in Joppa.
18. The family has numbered over 900: in August 1994, there were 482 children & adults.
19. Boys were admitted up till 1969, the last of whom completed their education in 1984.

THE SCOTS IN ULSTER:
THEIR DENIZATION AND NATURALISATION, 1605-1634

by Rev. David Stewart

PART I

It must be borne in mind that, prior to the year 1707, Scotland was a distinct Kingdom from England, governed by its own laws and possessing its own manners and customs. Scotsmen were aliens in the Dominion of the latter. From a very early period the incursions of Scots into Ulster, particularly those of the Islands and Highlanders, were a frequent occurrence, and many of them had succeeded in establishing themselves permanently in the northern counties, chiefly Antrim.

In the reign of Philip and Mary their Majesties addressed both house of the Irish Parliament, requesting them to adopt such measures as would discourage the Scots from seeking habitations in Ireland. In compliance with this regal command an Act was passed in 1556, prohibiting 'bringing in the Scots, retaining them, and marrying with them.'

While this Act was directed against those Scots referred to above, it was expressed in general terms to the exclusion of all the natives of that Kingdom. It remained operative during Elizabeth's reign, as her Majesty, like her predecessors, was averse to Scots acquiring possessions in her Dominion by prescriptive right. The explusion of the Scots was the chief object of the fruitless expeditions of Sir Thomas Smith and the Earl of Essex in 1573. Their services on the battlefields of Antrim and Clandeboy terminated, not in conquest, but in facilities to extend the olive branch of those whom they meant to evict.

The futile efforts of the two undertakers apparently induced her Majesty to adopt another method of dealing with the Scots in the hope of reducing them to subjection. Finding coercion of no avail, she abandoned rigour and endeavoured, by a pacific policy, to allure them into allegiance. To this end she issued a manifesto which sets forth her gracious intentions, and, at the same time, reveals the manner in which Denization was accomplished. She says:

'We are given to understand that a nobleman named 'Sorley Boy' [Macdonnell] and others, who be of the Scotch-Irish race, and some of the wild Irish, at this time are content to acknowledge our true and mere right to the countrie of Ulster and the crowne of Ireland, to profess due obedience to us and our crowne of England or Ireland, and to swear to be true subjects to us and our successors as other our natural subjects born in the English Pale be, or ought to be, submitting themselves to our laws and orders, upon condition that they may be received as denizens of England and Ireland; and we (being willing by all gentle means to bring the strayed sheep home again to the right fold, and to maintain peace and quietness, and to refuse none that will acknowledge their duty) are content to any 'meer Irish,' or Scotch-Irish, or other strangers who claim inheritance or shall hold any lands, or be resident in any place which is within our grant made to Sir Thomas Smith and Thomas, his son, now Colonel of the Ards and Clandeboye, who will be sworn to be true lieges to us and our successors (as denzien strangers to swear in the Chancery of England), before the said Thomas Smith, junior, or the Bishop of Down accompanied with other discreet persons, and from that day be content to hold their lands of us and the said Colonel, and shall yearly pay to us 20s for every plowland as all Englishmen, followers of the said Smith, pay, shall be reputed and taken for denziens, and not for 'meer Irish': and that the said Smith or the Bishop of Down may take the said Oath during the space of seven years; and, upon a certificate of the Colonel of any person or persons having taken the Oath, the Lord Deputy or Chancellor shall order letters of Denization to be passed to him or them (including twelve in each patent) if it shall be considered convenient.' April 14, 1573.

The Oath to be taken was as follows:

'Ye shall beare faith and true allegiance to the Queens' moost excellent majestie, Elizabeth, by the grace of God, and to her heirs and successors, Kings and Queens of England and Ireland, for the time being, all the daies of your life, as God shall helpe youe, and by the contents of this boke.' 1573.

Sorley was willing and he received a grant of denization and with it about two-thirds of the Glynns of Antrim. Dissatisfied with the latter he entered upon a policy which twelve years later terminated in a greatly extended grant and his complete submission.

For an alien to become an English subject it was necessary to obtain *ex donatione regis*, letters patent of Denization, pay a fine and take the Oath of Allegiance. As a denizen he occupied an intermediate position between an alien and a native born subject. He had the privilege of purchasing lands, but heirs born before the date of his Denization could not inherit in default of hereditary blood. Issue born after Denization of the father inherited to the exclusion of the others. This law, however, was changed in the reign of William III by an Act which permitted natural-born subjects to inherit as heirs to their ancestors though these were aliens.

A denizen, as such, was generally a person resolved to remain in Ireland and protect himself and his acquisitions by legal process. He could use the law courts but was unqualified to hold any office of trust, civil or military, and was incapable of receiving any grants from the Crown. Needless to say he was debarred from becoming a member of the Council or a Parliament.

Naturalisation, which was performed by Act of Parliament, put an alien in the same position as if he had been born a native subject. This was modified by a Statute of William III, which attached the limitations of denization to naturalisation for a period of seven years. At the end of this period all the privileges and obligations of citizenship were conferred. Denization is now obsolete and naturalisation is in the hands of the Home Secretary.

When James VI of Scotland succeeded Elizabeth as James I of England, and thus possessed both crowns, he was very desirous of uniting the two Kingdoms under one crown. However, he found that race, religion, laws, manners and customs contributed an insuperable barrier. He got no nearer this desired consummation than to style himself king of Great Britain and Ireland.

In the early years of his Majesty's reign as James I, many Lowland Scots passed over into Ulster to engage in the work of the new plantations. On these the king conferred naturalisation by the exercise of his prerogative. As early as November 22nd, 1605, he granted letters of naturalisation to Sir Hugh Montgomery prior to his settlement in the Ards. On August 18, 1607, he bestowed the same privilege on William Edmonston, James Edmonston, Archibald Haldan, David Bozwell, James Bozwell and some others, who designed to settle in Ulster.

At a later date, when arrangements had been made for the Plantation of Ulster, and before the law which excluded the Scots had been repealed, he followed the same course. The following Scots undertakers received grants of naturalisation in the year 1610. The first on the list is a specimen of the form used on each occasion.

Alexander Auchmootie, a patent of naturalisation and of the lands (lands specified)

John Auchmootie	June 24, 1610
Henry Acheson, Mid-Lothian	June 24, 1610
Michael Lord Burleigh, Pittendreich, Fifeshire	June 29, 1610
James Clapham, Servant in the Royal Household	Aug. 20, 1610
George Crawford, Laird of Lochenoreis, Ayrshire	Aug. 20, 1610
Cuthbert Cunningham, Glengarnock, Ayrshire	Sept. 19, 1610
James Cunningham, Laird of Glengarnock	July 20, 1610
John Cunningham, Crafield, Ayrshire	July 16, 1610
Sir James Douglas, Spott, Haddingtonshire	July 16, 1610
James Gibb, Servant in the Royal Household	Aug. 29, 1610
Robert Hamilton, of the Raploch family	Aug. 29, 1610
Robert Hepburn, of Aulderstown	July 12, 1610
Alexander McAula, of Durlin, Dumbartonshire	July 16, 1610
Robert Stewart, of Hilton, Edinburgh	Aug. 29, 1610
Sir Walter Stewart, of Minto, Teviotdale	July 20, 1610
William Sewart, Laird of Dundruff, Ayrshire	Aug. 29, 1610
William Stewart, brother of Viscnt, Garlies	Nov. 30, 1610

On January 29, 1612, naturalisation was granted to the following, all of whom settled in the barony of Dunluce on the estate of the Earl of Antrim

Boyd, Thomas	Stewart, John, alias McRobert
Dunlop, William	Stewart, John oge
Kennedy, Anthony	Stewart, Ninian
McNaughton, John	The last received naturalisation
McPhedrish, Gilbert	papers, January 18 1611/12
Stewart, Alexander	

Several of the others who received naturalisation at the King's royal hand:

Patrick Crawford, of Lifford	Sept. 30, 1611
Walter Logan, of Provstown, in the Ardes	May 18, 1614
Sir William Stewart, of Ramelton	July 7, 1613
William Wardlaw, of Lismullan, now Bishop's Court, Lecale, Co Down	May 18, 1614

In the year 1614, the Irish Parliament passed an Act in keeping with the spirit of Queen Elizabeth's manifesto, by which an alien of any nationality might take out denization papers and be constituted a subject, as his legitimisation proceeded *ex donatione regis*. On July 28, 1615, the King wrote to Chichester, the Lord Deputy, to act in this matter as his Commissioner. 'As many of the inhabitants of Scotland daily repair to Ireland' he is to grant them letters of denization. This Act conferred on the Scots Parliamentary sanction, which encouraged them to come in great numbers and settle in Ulster. Many thousands came over in a few years. Those who had arrived before the passing of the Act no doubt expected that, in time, such a law would be placed on the Statute book. The majority of the Scottish immigrants were farmers and labourers, the latter a class inclined to be troublesome. The Rev. Andrew Stewart of Donaghadee (1648-71), commenting on the character of the immigrants, says 'From Scotland came many and from England not a few, yet all of them generally the scum of both nations... And in a few years there flocked such a multitude of people from Scotland that these northern counties of Down, Antrim, Londonderry were, on a good measure planted, which had been waste before.'

Strange as it may appear, some Scots of substance, though long settled in Ireland, declined to abandon their nationality and, on specified terms, assume another. Such as Colonel David Boyd who came over with Sir Hugh Montgomery in 1606, and received from him a large estate in Ards 'for a valuable consideration'. Colonel Boyd died about the year 1623, 'being neither a denizen of Ireland or England'. His son and heir, Robert, was then a minor. According to law this estate should have been escheated to the Crown, but his Majesty generously declined from taking advantage of the Colonel's neglect 'on account of his good and faithful services.' Instead he directed that a commission should be appointed to find by inquisition what lands were purchased by the Colonel, and ordered that these should be passed to his son, Robert, without the imposition of a fine. This case alarmed the Scots and they petitioned his Majesty to take such action as would rescue them from their perilous situation.

In March 1625, the King wrote to the Lord Deputy, Falkland, saying that he had received a petition from the Scots station that for want of denization of themselves and those who had conveyed their estates to them they were advised that their estates were escheated, and they desired that Commissioners should be appointed that their holdings might be found for the King in order to his regranting them. His Majesty died on the 27th of this same month and was succeeded by his son, Charles I.

The papal party became very active soon after the accession of the young king. As advised by Falkland they offered a voluntary contribution of £120,000 to be paid in three years by quarterly instalments, if the king on his part would proclaim the 'graces' as an Act of State. The bounty was received, and the proclamation of the 'graces' issued, but these were never ratified by Parliament. The 'graces' were articles, fifty-one in number, most of which, if passed, would have removed many grievances of the Roman Catholics. One of the 'graces', number forty, was of special interest to the Scots, and in 1634 the Irish Parliament requested his Majesty to sanction it. 'That all Scotishmen, undertakers in Ulster, and in other places there, are to be made free denizens of that our Kingdom, and no advantage taken for want of denization against the heirs or assigns of those that be dead.'

To this Wentworth, Lord Deputy, better known as the Earl Stafford, generously added a rider as follows: 'We conceive it fit, if so please your Majesty, that there be a law not only for denization, but also for naturalisation.' This became law before the end of the year, and, in this manner, the Scots, on taking the oaths, were denized natural-born subjects, and were admitted to the full rights and privileges of Englishmen.

Sir George Radcliffe, in his biography of Strafford, enumerates this Act among the many good services performed by the sagacious and diligent Lord Deputy. He writes: 'He idenized all the *antenati* Scots which were born before Queen Elizabeth's death, a favour of very great advanatage to that nation'. Having said this he calls on them to 'remember how some of their countrymen reputed that benefit.'

The allusion here is to the active part taken by the Ulster Scots in the prosecution of the Earl of Stafford. 'A Petition from some Protestant inhabitants of the counties of Antrim, Down, Derry and Tyrone,' presented to the English Parliament, enumerates upwards of thirty grievances to which the Scots and Puritans of those regions were subjected during Stafford's administration. These form the bases of many of the accusations laid to the charge of the Lord Deputy. The full text of these grievances is given.

NOTES

1. Repealed by the Irish Parliament in 1615
2. Grants of denization were made on August 16 in the 26 of Elizabeth to Samuel and Daniel Molyneaux, natives of Bruges
3. Calendar of Patent and Close Rolls of Chancery: Morrin I, p.553
4. cf *Law Dictionary*, Tomlins, vol 1, and *Pocket Law Lexicon*, p. 131
5. All Scots, 'that they may be free from the yoke of servitude of Scotland, Ireland, or any other nation, and enjoy the rights and privileges of English subjects
6. Cal. of Pat. Rolls: James I
7. P. Adair, Narr. p.313
   'Amongst these, Providence sent over some worthy persons for birth, education and parts, yet the most part were such as either poverty, scandalous lives, or at the best, adventurous seeking or better accommodation set forward that way'. *Life of Robert Blair*, p.57.
   Writing about the praise service in the Church, Montgomery mentions the 'heedless vulgar' who disturbed the congregation with their clamorous tones. Mont. MSS. p.127
8. P Adair. Narr. p.3
9. Archdall's Lodge II, p.321
10. Cal. of Pat. Rolls: Charles I, Morrin, p.156
11. Cal. of Pat. and Rolls: James I
12. Strafford's Letters, II, p.434
13. Strafford's Letter, II, p.434

PART II

When Stafford granted facilities for a more ample naturalisation to the Scots he paid them a doubtful compliment in view of what happened this same year. It was in 1634 that he imposed the Service Book of the Church of England upon the Church of Ireland to the dissatisfaction of the Scots in general. Some of their ministers acquiesced so far as secured the emoluments of their parishes, but there was a minority who resolutely refused to submit. After frequent admonitions and solicitations they were deposed by legal process, whereupon they retired to Scotland followed by numerous members of their flocks.

Scotland at this period was in a ferment over a similar atrocity which the King and Laud had endeavoured to perpetrate upon their National Church. To frustrate their design the people renewed the National Convenant and resolved to stand together and resist, even by force of arms, this encroachment upon their spiritual liberty.

This was in 1638 and the following year Stafford imposed an oath on the Scots in Ulster binding those who took the same on no account to take up arms against the King. The administration of this oath (called *The Black Oath*) occasioned another exodus of Scots of spirit and integrity, who, despite all precautions of the Government found means of escaping to the homeland.

But worse followed in October 1641 when the native Irish, with terrifying suddenness, broke out in armed rebellion and slaughtered unsuspecting and defenceless men, women and children. The survivors rushed to the seaports, and again there was a great exodus of Scots, especially women and children.

However, the exodus was followed by an influx. In the summer of 1642 ten thousand Scottish soldiers arrived to quell the Irish in rebellion. Later, there were the Covenanters who sought in Ulster an asylum from the conquering Highlanders led by Montrose, and, to be brief, thousands who fled from persistent persecution during the reigns of Charles II and James II.

How naturalisation was carried out during this period of tumults and commotions, when the ebb and flow of population was almost continuous, is not recorded, but no doubt those who acquired real estate or other property had taken out naturalisation papers.

To begin with the County of Antrim, it is to be noted that the undertakers were Elizabethan Englishmen, to wit: – Conway, Chichester, Dobbs, Dalway, Hill, Langford, Clotworthy and Upton. Of these, Conway, Dobbs, and Hill were Episcopalians; and others were Puritans, and planted their lands largely with Englishmen of Puritan principles. Edmonston of Templecorran was a Scot who obtained his estate by purchase from Dalway, and Adair, another Scot, in the neighbourhood of Ballymena, also obtained his estate immediately. These two, as might have been expected, planted the lands under their authority with their own fellow-countrymen who came over in great numbers. Coalescence between them and the English of Puritan leanings was a natural outcome.

As has been often noted, all the land north of a line 'from the Curran of Larne to the Cutts of Coleraine' was the estate of the Earl of Antrim. This gentleman, though a Highlander and papist, had no objection to planting his dominion with Lowland Scots of the Reformed faith.

Early Scot Settlers in County Antrim

Adair, William, Kinhilt	Nov. 28, 1624
Blair, Alex	June 22, 1615
Blair, Hugh, Ballyshenog	Nov. 28, 1617
Blair, Marion, Inver, Larne	July 20, 1629
Barr, Robert, Belfast	1633
Boyd, Thomas, Carncoggy	Jan. 29, 1612
Boyd, Thomas, Ballyhacket	Feb. 9, 1625
Boyd, Robert, Inver, Larne	July 20, 1630
Bozwell, David, Templeougheragh	Aug. 18, 1607
Bozwell, James	Aug. 18, 1607
Brisbane, Elizabeth, wife of John Shaw, Ballygelly	Feb. .9, 1625
Burns, James, Carrickfergus	July 9, 1616
Buthill, David, Glandrine	June 22, 1615
Colville, Rev. Alexander, Ballymoney	Aug. 9, 1633
Cunningham, John, Loughrissoni, Co Antrim	Feb. 9, 1624
Dicke, Robert, Dunovernan	June 22, 1615
Dunbar, John, Carrickfergus	Nov. 28, 1617

Dunlop, Hugh, Mallagh	Feb. 9, 1625
Dunlop, Hugh, Inver, Larne	Jan. 20, 1633
Dunlop, William, (Balleken?)	Jan. 29, 1612
Edmonston, Alexander, Ardifracken	Nov. 28, 1617
Edmonston, William, Laird of Duntreath	Aug. 18, 1607
Ellis, Jane (nee Stewart), Carrickfergus	Nov. 28, 1617
Elllis, Margt., (nee Kennedy), Carrickfergus	Nov. 28, 1617
Fenton, William, minister of Cairncastle; owned	
Ballycreaghy, parish of Larne, and a house	
Newtown de Inver	Feb. 9, 1625
Futhie, Henry, clerk, Ra ?, Co Antrim	July 19, 1631
Fullerton, William, minister of Ballintoy,	
Archdeacon of Armagh	July 19, 1631
Haldane, Archibald	Aug. 18, 1607
Hamill, Matthew, Dunluce	June 22, 1615
Hamill, Robert, Magheraboy	June 22, 1615
Kilpatrick, Thomas, Carrickfergus	May 20, 1617
Kennedy, Anthony, Turnarobert, Armoy (d. 1625)	Jan. 29, 1612
Kennedy, David, Belfast	1633
Laderdeill, Janet, Newtown, Co Antrim	Feb. 9, 1625
Logan, Matthew, Bushmills	June 22, 1615
Luke, William, Ballyhebistock, Dervock	June 22, 1615
McAlexander, George, Ballyshanog	Nov. 28, 1617
McNaughton, John	Jan. 29, 1612
McNaughton, Alexander, Craigfreddock	June 22, 1615
McNaughton, John, Ballymaganog, Dunluce;	
agent for his cousin, the Earl of Antrim,	
(d. Mar. 10, 1630)	Aug. 29, 1611
McNeill, Hector, Culremony	Feb. .9, 1625
McPhedrish, Gilbert, Milnegowen, Caruglasmore	Jan. 29, 1612
Maxwell, John, Carrickfergus	May 20, 1617
Melvin, Jane, Ballymeaghan	Feb. 9, 1625
Millar, Agnes, Inver, Larne	July 20, 1629
Montgomery, Thomas, Carrickfergus	May 20, 1617
Monypenny, Andrew, Archdeacon of Connor	May 20, 1617
Niven, Robert, Belfast	1633

O'Greeve, Gilbert, Inver, Larne,	
(Name now 'Agnew'	Feb. 9, 1625
O'Greeve, John, Ballyhanpane	Feb. 9, 1625
Ross, Robert, Belfast	1633
Shaw, James, Ballygelly, Cairncastle	Feb. 9, 1625
Shaw, John, Ballygelly, Cairncastle	Feb. 9, 1625
Shaw, John, Carnfunnock, Corkermaine	Feb. 9, 1625
Shaw, William, Ballykilconan, Islandmagee	Nov. 28, 1617
Stewart, Alexander, Machremoire, Ramoan	Mar. 10, 1630
Stewart, Archibald, Ballyeatoe, Ballintoy	Feb. 9, 1624
Stewart, Alexander, Red Bay	Jan. 29, 1612
Streart, Christian, Corkermaine, Cairncastle	Feb. 9, 1625
Stewart, John, Red, Bay. His wife was Catherine, daughter of Ninian Stewart, Ballintoy, and their daughter, Janet, married Alexander Magee, Ballyuchan	Jan. 29, 1612
Stewart, John oge, Ballycloiske	Jan. 29, 1612
Stewart, Ninian, Ballintoy and Ballylough. The first settler on the Antrim coast. Died in 1621 and was succeeded by his son, Archibald	Jan. 18, 1612
Stewart, John McAndrew, Ballywilliam (Ballywillan?)	Aug. 9, 1633
Stewart, John oge, Ballyloist, Grange of Drumtullagh	Aug. 29, 1611
Thompson, Andrew	
Todd, Samuel, Layd, Co Antrim	1613
Trane, Bessy, Dunluce	Feb. 9, 1625
Tullis, Patrick, minister of Ramoan. Got a grant of Ballyriddery, Nov., 1622	Feb. 9, 1625
Wallace, William, minister of Portcoman (Dunluce; executor of the will of Wm Boyd, 1624)	Feb. 9, 1625

William Boyd of Dunluce, in his will dated Dec. 9, 1634 names his trusty friends:–
Dunlop, William, Laird of Crage in Scotland; Boyd, Thomas of Carnogie; and, Wallace, William, as his executors.

He also names his children, viz.: Adam, John, William, Katherine, Isabel, and Margaret. His sons were minors.

He also names his sisters, Isabel and Margaret; Kennedy, Walter, his son-in-law; Logan, John, his brother-in-law; Thompson, Robert, his servant; and David Thompson, his father. He also named:– Moneypenny, Andrew Archdeacon of Connor and Fenton, William, minister of Cairncastle, curators of his son Adam, to keep him at school; Dobbin, Anthony, owes him £60; Kennedy, Sir Wm., who is to get his best sword; Wallace, John his fowling piece.

Wallace, Margaret, LarneNov. 28, 1617

'Among the Scottish settlers on the lands of Sir Randal Macdonnell, soon after 1603, may be specially mentioned the Boyds, Browns, Dicks, Dunlops, Hamiltons, Hutchins, Kennedys, Macauleys, Mackays, Macnaghtons, Moores, Shaws, and Stewarts.'

Sir Foulke Conway's Estate, Original Settlers in Lisburn

Aphugh, Owen
Aprichard, John
Averne, William
Butterfield, Simon
Bland, Katherine
Bones, Robert
Browne, Robert
Burke, Francis
Calvert, Christopher
Cartwright, Jerome
Golly, John
Gouldsmith, Edward
Hollcote, Henry
Houseman, John
Howell, Richard
Leech, Humphrey
McNilly, John
Mace, John
Montgomery, Hugh
Morgan, Ann
Norris, John
O'Muldred, Peter
O'Murray, John
Palmer, Patrick
Paston, Thomas

Cloughanson, Henry
Cubbage, William
Dash, Humphrey
Date, Thomas
Davis, George
Dilworth, John
Dobbs, Maramduke
Dobbs, Richard
Edwards, William
Freeborne, Henry
Richardson, Stephen
Richardson, Simon
Rose, George
Savage, John
Glye, John
Smith, William
Stanton, Askulfe
Steward, Edward
Staffhard, Anthony
Symonson, Thomas
Tippen, John
Taylor, Robert
Walker, Richard
Warton, Robert
Wilson, Henric

The following are known to have resided in Co Antrim but there is no record of their naturalisation.

Strawbridge, Robert, d. 15 Aug. 1628, Dunluce
Ferly, Robert, 1617, Lisconnell
Gemell, John, 1621, Dunluce
Dunlapp, Brice, 1622, Cockermaine
Hutchone, George, 1622, Stranocum
Logan, John, 1619, Bushmills
McCawley, Brian Boy, 1612, Middle Glynnes
Kyd, Walter, 1630, Dunluce
Thompson, Rev. Andrew, ord. Ballywillan, 20 Dec.. 1615
Smith, Rev. Henry, Cairncastle, ord. 1629-30
Thompson, Rev. Laurence, Duneane, ord. priest, 1628
Kinnear, Rev. John, ord. p. 1626
Ritchie, Rev. Adam, Ramoan, ord. p. 1633
Dewar, Rev. David, Glenarm, ord. d. 1622
Lutfoot, Rev. David, Killagan, ord. p. 1630

County Armagh

Archeson, Archibald, Cloncarny	Feb. 12, 1619
Acheson, Henry, Coolemalish	July 20, 1610
Acheson, Patrick, son of Archibald	Feb. 12, 1619
Carcott, William, Drumcroine, Newry	Feb. 12, 1619
Cunningham, William, Drumcroine	Feb. 12, 1619
Douglas, Sir James, of Spott, Kut; gentleman of the Privy Chamber, Cloncarny	July 23, 1610
Maxwell, Robert, Dean of Armagh	May 20, 1617
Maxwell, Edward, Lisdrumchor, Loughgilly	Feb. 12, 1619
Richardson, Alexander, Ballyarkie (Ballyargon?)	Nov. 28, 1617
Sturgeon, Andrew, Corowmanin, Loughgilly	Feb. 12, 1619
Sturgeon, John, Creggans, Newry	Feb. 12, 1619
Watson, David, Rector of Killeavey	May 20, 1617
Walshe, John, Merchant	Nov. 28, 1617
Walker, Archibald, Merchant	Nov. 28, 1617
Wilson, Robert, Lisnagat	Feb. 12, 1619

From other sources

Lauder, William, 1617
Montgomery, Robert, Edenacaanany   Nov. 28, 1617

Tennants of John Hamilton, Esq, Hamiltonsbawn, 1617

Allen, John	Gilmore, Patrick	Dowling, Edward
Allen, Robert	Granton, Patrick	Johnston, John
Arkles, David	Greer, Cuthbert	Kennedy, Gilbert
Bell, Andrew	Greer, Eliza	Kirk, John
Bell, William	Grier, Alexander	Leitch, David
Brown, John	Grier, Archibald	McKernan, Cornelius
Carothers, Francis	Grindall, Henry	Moffatt, James
Calte, Adam	Grinidell, Ralph	Parker, George
Davidson, John	Hall, John	Pringle, Thomas
Deans, John	Hamilton, John	Rae, Adam
Elliott, Robert	the elder, Dromanish	Ritchie, Patrick
Ferguson, John	Hamilton, John sen	Shirloe, Lawrence
Ferguson, Robert	Hamilton, John	Syne, Alexander
Flack, Fergus	Hamilton, Robert	Trimble, John
Gamble, George	Hamilton, Robert	Wilkie, John
Gamble, Matthew	Hope, Matthew	

County Cavan

Aughmooty, Alexander, Drumheada	June 4, 1610
Aughmooty, John, Keylagh	June 27, 1610
Bailie, William, Bailieborough	June 2, 1629
Creighton, Thomas, Aghabane	June 9, 1617
Hamilton, Francis, Keelough Castle	Feb. 12, 1619
Hamilton, Jane (wife of above)	Feb. 12, 1619
Hamilton, John, Coronary	July 29, 1629
Lother, Alexander, Clony	Feb. 12, 1619
Lother, George, Derrinrehed	Feb. 12, 1619
Taylor, Robert, Minister, Kilcan	May 20, 1617

William Bailie's Freeholders
Bailie, Edward, held Drumlyne, commonly called Lisgar: Dirrymore
Bailie, James, held Molepalagh and Lisnolsk

William Bailie's Leaseholders

Bailie, John

Barbour, David

Cuthbertson, Gilbert

Hamilton, John

Miller, Walter

Rae, William

Stevenson, John

Tate, James

Generally their leases were of seventy-one years duration.

Lord Claneboy's Tenants Parish of Clouke

Kennedy, John – In 1616 Lord Claneboy granted to him and his heirs forever the lands of Cashel, Kappagh, and Lurgaboye

Bailie, Edward – On 2 April, 1627, Corlatcurroll, for three lives

Coch, John – On 14 April, 1627, Lisnaclea, for his natural life

Price, William – 10 April, 1627, Corvillemahie, for his natural life

Steele, George – 10 April, 1627, Cornelyon, for his natural life

Stewart, James – 15 April, 1627, Coreagh, for his natural life

John Hamilton's Tenants, (Kilcloghan Proportion)

Barber, David – fee-farm

McCullough, David – fee-farm

John Hamilton's Leaseholders (Kilcloghan Proportion)

Anderson, Alexander – Knocknelosky, lease for 21 years	April 16, 1619
Davyson, Alexander – Glasdmonan, lease for life	Dec. 2, 1618
Deans, John – Rouskie, lease for seven years	May 1, 1620
Finlay, John & Pat. – Tullylurkan, lease for 7 years	May 12, 1620
Musgrave, John – Ralaghan, lease for 21 yrs	May 1, 1618
Taylor, Robert – Latsibourgidan, lease for life	April 9, 1619
Udney, Oliver – Cran, lease for five years	April 1, 1621
Wylie, John – Kilnecrene, lease for 21 years	April 16, 1627

Co Donegal

Adair, Archibald, Dean of Raphoe	Nov. 28, 1617
Allen, Robert, Raphoe, Denization granted	Nov. 28, 1617
Alexander, Sir William	Nov. 28, 1617
Barkley, Robert, Figart, Raphoe	Nov. 28, 1617
Barry, James, Raphoe	Nov. 28, 1617
Bauld, Archibald, Airdrie, par. of All Saints	Nov. 28, 1617
Blair, Hugh, Ballyshenog	Nov. 28, 1617

Brisbane, John, Gortlush, par. of All Saints	July 9, 1617
Bruce, John, Drumacrin, Inishamacsaint	Nov. 1617
Bruce, Thomas, DD, Clericus, Raphoe	Sept. 12, 1629
Buchanan, William, Doonan, Killymand	Nov. 1617
Burne, James, Rathmullan	Nov. 1617
Campbell, Colin, Rathmullan	Nov. 28, 1617
Campbell, John, Ballyekeringe, Killteenvogue	Nov. 28, 1617
Carr, James, Rathmullan	Nov. 28, 1617
Carr, John, Rathmullan	Nov. 28, 1617
Carr, Edward, Rathmullan	Nov. 28, 1617
Cloggie, John, Carntoolagh, Killybegs	Aug. 17, 1617
Colquhoun, Daniel, Corkagh	May 20, 1617
Colquhoun, Robert, Corkagh	July 14, 1630
Coohoone, Andrew, Droughedonan	Nov. 28, 1617
Coohoone, Peter, Droughedonan	Nov. 28, 1617
Crawford, William, Droughedonan	Nov. 28, 1617
Cunningham, Alexander, minister of Inver	Aug. 17, 1617
Cunningham, Sir James, Portlagh	July 20, 1610
Cunningham, Lady Katherine (wife of above)	Aug. 17, 1627
Cunningham, Joan, widow of James Cunningham, Gortree	Nov. 28, 1624
Cunningham, James, Barony of Raphoe (Fort Cunningham)	May 29, 1629
Cunningham, James, Ballyaghan	Aug. 17, 1616
Cunningham, Sir John, Ardee	July 16, 1610
Cunningham, Lady Jean, wife of Sir john	Nov. 28, 1624
Cunningham, William	July 19, 1631
Cunningham, William	July 9, 1616
Cunningham, John, Esq, Raphoe	Aug. 7, 1616
Cunningham, John, Manorcunningham	May 23, 1629
Cunningham, Patrick, Portlough	Nov. 28, 1617
Cunningham, Patrick, Imlick, Killea	Nov. 28, 1625
Cunningham, William, Gortinleve, All Sts	Nov. 28, 1617
Dick, James, Raphoe	Nov. 28, 1617
Dougal, Alexander, Rathmullan	Nov. 28, 1617
Ewart, John, Dunmoyle, Stranorlar	1629
Fleming, John, Raphoe	Nov. 28, 1617

Forecheade, James, Castruse, All Saints	Nov. 28, 1617
Fulton, John, Beltany, Raphoe	Nov. 28, 1617
Galbreth, James, senr, Taboyne	Aug. 17, 1616
Galbreth, James, junr, Taboyne	Aug. 17, 1616
Glass, Alaster, Figart, Raphoe	Nov. 28, 1617
Glen, John, Lifford	Aug. 17, 1617
Gordon, Sir Robert, Boylagh & Banagh	Dec. 2, 1615
Hall, James, Raphoe	Aug. 17, 1617
Hamilton, Alexander, Tullynaghdonnell, Raphoe	Nov. 28, 1617
Hamilton, Claude, Raphoe	Aug. 17, 1616
Hamilton, John Raphoe	Nov. 17, 1616
Hamilton, John, Loughesk	July 19, 1631
Hamilton, Thomas, Rathmullan	Nov. 1617
Hamilton, William, Trenta, Taughboyne	July 9, 1617
Hamilton, William, Loughnakey, Tullyfern	Aug. 17, 1616
Hamilton, widow Joan, widow of James Cunningham, Gortree	Nov. 28, 1625
Hamilton, Robert, gent., Carricklee, Urney	Aug. 17, 1617
Hamilton, William, gent., Ballyfattin, Urney	Aug. 17, 1617
Hamilton, William, gent., Loughskeine	Aug. 17, 1617
Henrison, Alexander, Rathmullan	Nov. 28, 1617
Henry, John, Raphoe	Nov. 28, 1617
Hunter, Robert, Cargin	Aug. 17, 1616
Johnston, James, Ballyheglis	Nov. 28, 1617
Julius, Alexander	Sept. 22, 1619
Kennedy, David, Monclink	May 20, 1617
Kernes, Alexander, Termakine	Nov. 28, 1617
Kilpatrick, Archibald, Teevickmoy	1629
Kilpatrick, Robert, Teevickmoy	1629
Knox, Andrew, Bishop of Raphoe	Sept. 22, 1619
Laycock, Thomas Lifford	Aug. 17, 1617
Leckie, Robert, Clashigowan	May 20, 1617
Leslie, John, Bp of Raphoe, made a free denizen	July 1, 1632
Lindsay, James, Magevlin	July 16, 1610
McAuld, Alex., Ballyreagh	July 16, 1610
McCamuel, Gawen, Dromanan	Aug. 17, 1616
McClairne, John, Raphoe	Nov. 28, 1617

McCullough, Thomas, Doonan, Killymard	Aug. 17, 1616
McKinney, Alexander, Rathmullan	Nov. 28, 1617
McLintagh, Alexander, Ratean, Taughboyne	Nov. 28, 1617
McLornan, Wm, Moynevonnen	Nov. 28, 1624
McMath, Andrew, Donegal	Nov. 28, 1617
McMath, Archibald, Teevickmoy, Stranolar	Jan. 1629
Machell, William, Damcliffe, Killymard	Nov. 28, 1617
Machen, James, Drumcarne	May 20, 1617
Maxwell, James, Dunmoyle, Stranolar	1629
Moore, John, Raphoe	Nov. 28, 1617
Montgomery, Robert, Moneglasse	Nov. 28, 1617
Moorhead, William, Ballyheglis	Nov. 28, 1617
Murray, John (later Earl of Annandale)	Dec. 13, 1620
Nelson, William, Rathmullan	Nov. 28, 1617
Nesbit, James, Tullaghdonnell, Raphoe	Nov. 28, 1617
Orr, James, Raphoe	Nov. 20, 1617
Patterson, Matthew, Figart, Raphoe	Nov. 28, 1617
Patoun, William*, ministerum verbi Dei apud ecclesiam Rathmoithie (Raymoghry)	1616

*William Patton, ordained priest 1613. He was M.A., and came from Irvine Inst. Clonmany, Dioc. of Derry, Jan. 19, 1630. of Leslie's Clergy Lists

Pont, Robert, Ramelton	Feb. 12, 1619
Rankin, Wm	Aug. 17, 1616
Ritchie, John, merchant, Carntullagh, Killybegs	Aug. 17, 1617
Robson, Patrick, Figart, Raphoe	Nov. 28, 1617
Sawyer, James, Moynegragan	Nov. 28, 1624
Scott, Patrick, Ray	Nov. 28, 1625
Sempell, Robert, Carrickballydoney	May 20, 1617
Semple, Sir John, Letterkenny	Jan. 27, 1617
Semple, Andrew, Ballyheglis	Nov. 28, 1617
Semple, Brice	Sept. 22, 1629
Semple, Julius	Sept. 22, 1629
Simpson, Robert, carpenter, Raphoe	Nov. 28, 1617
Smith, John, Raphoe	Aug. 17, 1617

Smith, John, Figart, Raphoe	Nov. 28, 1617
Smith, John, Oboyleston	Aug. 17, 1616
Spence, Robert, Rathmullan	Nov. 1617
Stephenson, Alexander, Raphoe	Aug. 17, 1617
Stevin, John, Figart, Raphoe	Nov. 1617
Stewart, Alexander, Ballenembeg	Nov. 28, 1617
Stewart, Alexander, Loghy, Drumholm	July 9, 1617
Stewart, Alexander, Ballyheglis	Nov. 28, 1617
Stewart, John, Killaghtie	Nov. 1617
Stewart, John, Lismoghry, Ray	Nov. 1617
Stewart, Anthony, Drumoghill	May 20, 1617
Stewart, George	July 19, 1617
Stewart, Matthew	July 19, 1631
Stewart, John, Ballyreagh	May 9, 1629
Stewart, John, Veagh	Nov. 28, 1624
Stewart, Sir Walter, Corkey	July 20, 1610
Stewart, Wm, gent., Cooleaghy	Aug. 29, 1610
Stewart, John, son of Alexander, of Ballylawn, progenitors of the Marquis of Londonderry, was granted denization	May 9, 1629
Cf. Hill's *Plant. in Ulster*, p.511	
Stewart, William, Laird of Dunduff	Aug. 9, 1629
Thomson, James, Lifford	Aug. 17, 1617
Vance, John, Clericus, Kilmacrennan	Nov. 1617
Wilson, James, Letterkenny	Nov. 1617
Witherspoon, Andrew, Lifford	Aug. 17, 1617
Wood, Andrew, Maymore, Taughboyne	Nov. 1617
Wood, James, Maymore, Taughboyne	Nov. 1617
Young, Robert, Culdrum	Nov. 28, 1624

Sir John Cunningham's Tenants
November 1st, 1614
Airdrie:-

Bernard Hunter	John Martin	James Robin

Moyle:-
William Boyle

Monegragane:–
Alexr. McIlchany   James Patterson   John Plowright
Moyfadda:–
James Boyle   Wm Cunningham   John Ramsay
John Bryce   John Flemminge   William Sare
Andrew Calwell   Donnell Gillaspick John Wigton
Alexr. Calwell   Wm McCassick   Stephen Woolson
Bernard Cunningham   Donnell McEvene
Plaister:–
Robert Allen   Donnell McKilmun   John Wilson
John Fyieff   John Molsed
Dunboy:–
Robert Boyd   Andrew Cunningham and 5/16th part of
Roughan, adjoining Monegragane to Donnell Connell
Cf. *Ulster Inquisitions*, Donegal (5), Car. I

James Cunningham's Tenants, May 1, 1613
Dyan (? Dryan):– Donnell, McErdy; John Roger; William Teyse (?
Tees)
Eredy:– John Alexander; Andrew Arnett; William Arnett; John
Hamilton; Edward Homes; John Hutchine; George Leitch; Peter
Stevenson
Grackhy:– David Kennedy; Hugh Moore; Wm Moore; Wm.
Valantyne
Magherybeg:– John Brown; John Harper; Hugh Lockhard; Thos.
Scott; John Purveyance
Magherymore:– George Black; Andrew Brown; Wm Ekyn; Wm
Gaate (? Galt); Jas. Gilmore; John McKym; Robt. Patterson; Geo.
Peere (? Pery); Wm Rankin; Andrew Smythe; John Smythe; William
Sutherland; John Watson
Moyagh:– Alexander Dunne; John Dunne; John Dunne, junr;
Alexander Grynney; William Hendry; Donnell McKym; William
Stewart; John Young
Tryaucarrickmore:– David Kennedy and Wm.Valentine.
Cf. *Ulster Inquisitions*, Donegal (5), Car. I

Tenants of William Stewart, Laird of Dunduff – June 10, 1614
Drumalis, one-third of; – Michael McLoghery, Owen Macintyre

Drumbarnard:– John Cunningham alias Huggin, Jas. Dunsayer, Wm Fullerton, John Hood, Gilbert Kennedy and Archibald Thompson
Drumoghill:– Arthur Stewart, gent
Manechant:– Hugh O'Dogherty; Con. O'Donnell
Mondowy:– James Maghan; Toole McVegany; Dermot O'Brallaghan; Shane O'Brallaghan; Kilgroome O'Derny; Anthony Stewart, gent
Moneymore:– Alexr. Hunter; Alexr. Lockard; James McKay; James Sayne; William Smelley; John Smyth; Walter Stewart
Kilvarry:– Thomas Lodge

County Down

The plantation of this county was begun a few years before the scheme known as *The Plantation of Ulster* was devised. In 1605 two Ayrshire Scots obtained grants of land on a princely scale compared with the mean 'proportions' of the Plantation Scheme. These two enterprising Scots were followed by such numbers of their compatriots that in 1610 Montgomery was to march a thousand 'able fighting men' before the king's muster-master.

Probably Hamilton could have done better as he had a larger estate. By purchase, he had added the Barony of Dufferin to his grant. In the muster of 1631 he paraded 1,776 men compared with 1,317 presented by Montgomery. Together they numbered 3,093 out of a total of 4,045 enrolled in the County of Down. In May also, it may be noted that of the 13,095 men enrolled in the nine counties of Ulster, this county furnished almost one-third of the number and most of these were Scots.

Estate of Hugh Montgomery, Lord of Ards

Agnew, Andrew, Carneyhill	May 20, 1617
Agnew, Thomas, Greyabbey	May 20, 1617
Aicken, John, Donaghadee	May 20, 1617
Allen, Patrick, Ballydoonan, Donaghadee	May 20, 1617
Anderson, David, Castleavery, Scrabo	Nov. 28, 1617
Barkley, John, Ballyrolly, Donaghadee	May 20, 1617
Barcklie, David – ?	Feb. 18, 1622
Barcklie, Elizabeth nee Cunningham)	Feb. 18, 1622
Blair, Beatrix (nee Hamilton), wife of Rev. Robt.	
Blair, Bangor	1632

Boyd, Thomas, Cronshown, Newtownards	May 20, 1617
Boyle, Robert, Drumfad, Donaghadee	May 20, 1617
Brackley, Ninian, Newtownards	May 20, 1617
Cathcart, James, Ballyrogan, Newtownards	May 20, 1617
Catherwood, William, Ballyfrenis, 1606	May 20, 1617
Cooper, James, Ballychosta (?Ballyhaskin)	May 20, 1617
Crawford, John, Ballyatwood	May 20, 1617
Crawford, William, Cunningham	May 20, 1617
Cunningham, Alexander, Ringcreevy, Comber, 1623	May 20, 1617
Cunningham, Claude, Donaghadee	May 20, 1617
Cunningham, David, Drumfad, Donaghadee	May 20, 1617
Cunningham, George, Esq., Loughriscouse, M.P. for Newtownards, 1613	May 20, 1617
Cunningham, Hugh, Castlespie, Tullynakill	May 20, 1617
Cunningham, John, Ringcreevy, father of Alexander	May 20, 1617
Cunningham, William, Donaghadee	May 20, 1617
Cunningham, John, Loughriscouse	Feb. 9, 1624/25
Drummond, Malcolm, Ballywatticock	May 20, 1629
Edmonston, Archibald, Ballybrian, Greyabbey	July 3, 1631
Frazer, John, Donaghadee	May 20, 1617
Harper, John, Donaghadee	May 20, 1617
Harper, John, Ballyhay, Donaghadee	May 20, 1617
Harvey, Thomas, Newtownards	Nov. 28, 1617
Hunter, William, Ballydoonan, Donaghadee	May 20, 1617
Leckey, Christina, alias McClelland, wife of Malcolm Drummond, Ballywatticock	Nov. 28, 1625
Drummond, William, Ballywatticock	Nov. 20, 1625
McDowgall, Uthred, Ballymaconnell	May 20, 1617
McMakene, James, Donaghadee	May 20, 1617
Montgomery, Lady Elizabeth	Feb. 18, 1622
Montgomery, Sarah (nee Maxwell) Viscountess Ards	Nov. 28, 1626
Montgomery, Hugh, 1st Viscount	Nov. 22, 1605
Montgomery, Hugh, Granshaw, Donaghadee, son of John, who, with his family were murdered by wood-kerne	May 20, 1617
Montgomery, Lady Jean, wife of Hugh, son and	

heir to Lord Montgomery, and eldest daughter of Sir William Alexander, Secretary of State for Scotland	Nov. 28, 1626
Montgomery, John, Ballynacross, Donaghadee	May 20, 1617
Montgomery, Matthew, Donaghadee	Nov. 28, 1617
Montgomery, Patrick, Craigboy, Donaghadee	May 20, 1617
Montgomery, Robert, Ddonaghadee	May 20, 1617
Moore, Hector, Ballydoonan, Donaghadee	May 20, 1617
Moore, William, Milntown (Drumbo?)	May 20, 1617
Moore, William, preacher, Newtownards	Nov. 28, 1617
Mowlane, John, Cronstown, Newtownards	May 20, 1617
Montgomery, Wm., Donaghadee	May 20, 1617
Moon, Jn., Donaghadee	May 20, 1617
Nevin, Thomas, Ballycopeland, 1606	May 20, 1617
Peacock, John, Ballydoonan, Donaghadee, and Tullykevin, Greyabbey	May 20, 1617
Shaw, John, Ganaway & Ballyhasker, 1616	May 20, 1617
Shaw, Patrick, Ballywalter	May 20, 1617
Shaw, William, Ballyquhosk (? Ballyhasker)	May 20, 1617
Spier, Alexander, Greyabbey	Nov. 28, 1617
Thomson, John, Blackabbey	May 20, 1617
Thomson, John ——?	Feb. 12, 1619
Wilson, Allen, Newtownards	Nov. 28, 1617
Wylie, John, Ballyhay, Donaghadee	May 20, 1617
Wyms, William, Newtownards	May 20, 1617
Wilson, Robt., Newtownards	May 20, 1617

From other sources:
Boyd, Col. David, Ballycastle, Greyabbey, 1606
Catherwood, William, Ballyfrenis, 1606
Cowper, James, Ballychosta (?Ballyhaskin), 20 May, 1617
Cunningham, Alexander, Ringcreevy, Comber, 1623

Cunningham, George, Esq., Loughriscouse, M.P. for Newtownards	1613

Kennedy, Fergus, Ballyloughan, Comber
Kennedy, Hugh, Greengaves, Newtownards
McCashin, John, Ballymurphy, Greyabbey, 1607

McCashin, Hugh, Ballygrangee, Greyabbey, 1629
McDowell, Sir John, Ballystockard
Montgomery, Adam, carpenter
Montgomery, Adam, gent, Ballyalton, Comber, 1610
Montgomery, Hugh, Islandmore, Greyabbey, 1629
Montgomery, John, Ballyrolly, Donaghadee
Montgomery, Thomas, Newtownards
Montgomery, William, Ballyhaft, Newtownards
Montgomery, William, Donaghadee, 1620, writer, burges of Irvine
(Cf. *Hist. Coll. of Ayr IX* p.95)
Moore, Patrick, came over with Sir Hugh Montgomery
Orr, James, Ballyblack, d. 1627

In other Districts of Co. Down
Wardlaw, Archibald, Drumcaw, Kinelarty. died in 1657
Wardlow, William, Lismullan, Lecale. Died in 1641
(Cf. *Ul. Jour. Arch. I*, p.93)

Scots on other Estates in Ards

Adair, Gilbert, Archine, Ardquin	May 20, 1617
Echlin, John, Ardchine, Ardquin	Feb. 9, 1625
Echlin, John, Ballyphillip	July 19, 1631
Echlin, Margaret, Archine, Ardquin	Feb. 9, 1625
Howson, Wm and his wife Katherine Vaus, Portaferry	Nov. 28, 1625
McDougal, Patrick, Portaferry	Nov. 28, 1625
Monypenny, Arthur, Portaferry	Nov. 20, 1625
Seton, Janet, Archine, Ardkeen	Feb. 9, 1625
Echlin, Robert, M.A., St Andrew's, Bishop Down and Connor	May 18, 1613

Unidentified:

Stanhouse, William, Carbolzie	May 20, 1617
Wilson, Robert, Lisnagada	Feb. 12, 1619

Undenized
Boyd, Col. David, Ballycastle, Greyabbey, 1606
Estate of Lord Claneboy

Abercrombie, Thomas, Whitechurch (Ballywalter)	July 5, 1631
Adair, Alexander, Ballymaghan, Holywood	Nov. 11, 1625

Adair, William, he and his wife Catherine Cathcart, and their sons, Robert and William, Ballymughan	Nov. 11, 1625
Adams, Daniel, Ballymullan, Bangor	Nov. 28, 1617
Bailie, Edward, Ringdufferin, 1636	July 5, 1631
Blair, Alexander, Bangor	Nov. 28, 1617
Boyd, David, Glastry	May 20, 1617
Carmichael, Rachel, Ballywalter	July 5, 1631
Craig, Michael, Roddens, Inishargie, 1616	May 20, 1617
Cunningham, Adam, Balligan, Innishargie	Nov. 28, 1617
Cunningham, Alexander, Ballysallagh, Minor, 1615	Nov. 28, 1620
Gemmil, John, Ballymullan, Bangor	Nov. 28, 1617
Glen, James, East Holywood	Nov. 28, 1617
Greenshields, William, Ballygrainey, Bangor	May 20, 1617
Hamilton, Archibald, brother of Lord Claneboy, Ballygrat, Bangor, 1616	May 20, 1617
Hamilton, Gawn, Ballyminitragh, Bangor	May 20, 1617
Barcklie, David, Ladyland, Killyleagh	Nov. 20, 1617
Danielston, Charles, Provenston (Priesttown, Ardquin)	May 20, 1617
Hamilton, George, Ballymaghan	May 20, 1617
Hamilton, James, Ballywalter	July 5, 1631
Hamilton, John, brother of Lord Claneboy, Ballyrobert and Ballydavey, 1616	May 20, 1605
Hamilton, Patrick, and Eliza his wife. He was brother of Lord Claneboy, Granshaw, Comber	July 5, 1631
Hamilton, Robert, Ballynicholl, Comber	Nov. 28, 1617
Hamilton, Hugh, Ballymenock	May 20, 1617
Hamilton, John, Balligan	May 20, 1617
Hamilton, William, Bangor	Nov. 28, 1617
Hamilton, William, Rubane	July 5, 1617
Hamilton, William, Ballyclochan	May 20, 1617
Harper, Robt., Priesttown, Ardquin	May 20, 1617
Hogg, Robert, Ballyleidy, Bangor	Nov. 28, 1617
Howie, James, Ballymullan, Bangor	Nov. 28, 1617
Julius, Alex., Kinalarty	Sept. 22, 1619
Kelso, Thomas, Ballyhackamore, 1616	Nov. 28, 1617
Kennedy, George, Bangor	Nov. 28, 1617

Kennedy, Oliver, Rowbane	July 5, 1631
Kennedy, Anthony, Ballyminitragh	Nov. 28, 1617
Kennedy, David, Portavilly (Killeen, Dundonald)	Nov. 28, 1617
Kylr, Robert, Ballymenoch	Nov. 28, 1617
Lindsay, John, Ballymullan	Nov. 28, 1617
Logan, Walter, Priesttown, Ardquin	May 20, 1617
McDougall, Uchtred, Ballymaconnell	May 20, 1617
McIlveyne, David, Balligan	Nov. 28, 1617
Martin, John, Dunneville (? Dunover)	Nov. 28, 1617
Maxwell, Edward, Dunover, 1616	May 20, 1617
Maxwell, James, Granshaw, Inishargie	May 20, 1617
Maxwell, John, Ballyhalbert	May 20, 1617
Moneypenny, Andrew, Prebendary of St Andrews	May 20, 1617
Montgomery, John, Roddens, Innishargie	May 20, 1617
Moore, Robert, Whitechurch, Ballywalter	July 5, 1631
Moore, William, Ballybregagh, Killinchy	July 5, 1631
Moore, Jane, Ballybregagh, Killinchy (wife)	July 5, 1631
O'Hamill, Groomsport, home 'Manus'	Nov. 28, 1617
O'Hamill, Neill, Ballyhemlin, Ballyhalbert	Nov. 28, 1617
Peebles, John, Carrow John Bostie, Inishargie	Nov. 28, 1617
Reid, Andrew, Ballymullan, Bangor	Nov. 28, 1617
Ross, James, Ballyminitragh, Bangor	Nov. 28, 1617
Reynolds, Paul, Bangor, M.P. for Killyleagh	July 5, 1617
Ross, Robert, Ballyfatherly	Nov. 28, 1617
Semple, Andrew, Ballygrainey, Bangor	Nov. 28, 1617
Stevenson, William, Bangor	Nov. 28, 1617
Stanehouse, Wm., Corbally, Killyleagh	May 20, 1617
Waddell, Alexander, Ballymenock, Holywood	Nov. 28, 1617
Wallace, William, Ballyobican, Inishargie	May 20, 1617
Wanchop, James, Ballygraffan, Ballyhalbert	Nov. 28, 1617
Williamson, James, Clea, Killyleagh	May 20, 1617
Wilson, John, Bangor	Nov. 28, 1617

From other sources:

Bailie, Alexander – Inishargie, cir. 1620
Blackwood, John – Bangor
Blair, Rev. Robert – Bangor, 1623

Carlile, George – witnessed a deed 1623
Cathcart, William – witnessed a deed 1621
Cunningham, Hugh – Castlespie, witnessed a deed 1621
Dunbar, James – Toyle. Fee-farm 1621
Hilton, William – witnessed a document, 1623
Kennedy, John – servant to Lord Clonaboy, 1616
Maxwell, John – Ballyeasborough, Ballyhalbert, 1623
O Dornan, James – Groomsport, at will, 1616
O'Gilmore, Toole – Ballysallagh, Bangor, 1616
O'Hamil, Jenkin – Knocknagoney
O'Mulcreve, Owen – part of Ballysallagh, 1616
Robb, John – Land surveyor, Carrowreagh
Stewart, John – Ballymoran, Killinchy, cir. 1620
Trail, Lt-Col. James – Tollychin, Killyleagh, 1633
Ross, James and Robert – Ballyminitragh, Bangor, were the sons of
Alexander Ross of Irvine, Ayrshire. They were subsequently known
as Ross of Portavoe
(Cf. *Arch. Coll. of Ayrshire, IX*, p.276)
Watson, John – Schoolmaster at Bangor, 1620
(Cf. *Arch. Coll. of Ayrshire, IX*, p.255)

Tenants on the Estate of Lord Claneboy
(Taken from the Maps drawn by Thomas Raven in 1625)

These maps, upwards of seventy in number, set forth in townlands only a portion of his lordship's great estate.

Comparatively few of these maps bear the names of the occupying tenants, and the contrast between these and the vacant ones suggest, at first sight, that the latter were untenanted. The explanation probably is that those devoid of names were the feefarm and the terminable estate of tacksmen or middlemen whose rent-roll was no concern of his lordship or his topographer.

In the Hamilton *Mss* (page 36) the author states that his lordship 'in managing his estates was careful and wary in giving inheritances or leases above three lives, and went that length but with very few'. It is noticeable that the townlands bearing the names of tenants are chiefly in the vicinity of Bangor and Killyleagh at each of which his lordship had a residence. It was the desire of the Government that, in those early days of the Plantation, landlords should have a store of arms in their castles, and that they should be surrounded by a substantial body of tenants who would be readily available to use them in suppressing any acts of hostility or rebellion on the part of the natives.

The following are the names of the tenants inscribed on the maps of 1625.

Bangor and Vicinity:

Mr Austin-65 acres

Alexander Blair-

Saunders Hamilton-

Saunders Blair-

Arch. Dunlop-32 acres

John Forsith-2 acres

Gawn Hamilton-73 acres

Wm Hamilton-35 acres

Andrew Lindsay-29 acres

James Logan-

Ba.. McGee-

Alex. McLellan-19 acres

John McLellan-35 acres

Thomas McLellan-5 acres

David Montgomery-

Archibald Monett-3 acres

James Nesbit-

Gabriel Pollock-3 acres

Ballyskelly:

Andrew Crawford-117 acres

William Magee-55 acres

Bessie Rudd-20 acres

George Rudd-58 acres

Ballygilbert:

Daniel Adams-113 acres

Edward Bayly-107 acres

Quintin Hamilton-59 acres

William Nesbit-38 acres

Ballymagee:

James Anderson-11 acres

Archibald Dunlop-3 acres

Ochtred McDowell-6 acres

John McMillin-39 acres

Robert Murray-39 acres

Ballymaconnell and Ballyholm:

Widow Allen-53 acres

John Boyd-20 acres

Owen Boyd-2 acres

John Dunlop-6 acres

Janet Dunbar-22 acres

William Galt-22 acres

William Hamilton-6 acres

Ballyminitragh:

Anthony Kennedy-131 acres

Robert Kyle-66 acres

Saunders Stevenson-74 acres

Kennistown and Toddstown:

Helen Dunlop-27 acres   Nichol McLellan-34 acres

Ballysallagh Union:
Saunders Cunningham-220 acres, fee-farm

Parish of Dundonald
Lisbredan – James Hamilton, 75 acres
Ballyrainey – Thomas McIlwrath, 70 acres; Widow Lloyd
Unicarvel – Thomas Keevet, 27 acres; George Mathyson, 48 acres
Ballyloran – Robert Hamilton, 79 acres; Thomas Hare, 100 acres
Ballybeen – Saunders Dickson, 75 acres, William Dunlop, 71 acres

Parish of Comber
Ballynichol:–
Robert Brown   James McEwen
James McCartney   James McKee
Cattogs:–
Adam Hamilton   Robert Hamilton-20 acres
Carnesure:
Walter Douglas-69 acres
Town and Parks of Killyleagh
Mr John Boyle   Duncan Read
Widow Crear (Greer?)   John Ross
Andrew Harvey   George Scott
Robert Hogg   John Stewart
James Moore   Thomas Watson
William Moore   John Welsh
Edward O'Coffie   ——? Wylie
His brother (O'Coffie)   James Young
John Paddin (Junr)
Rathcunningham – Robert Hamilton

Ballea
The following were inhabitants of his parish in 1641 and probably
prior to that fateful year.
William Kuming, Senr; Marion Tate, his wife; William, John and
Charles, their sons
John Millar, who lived near the church
Com. Maxwell; John Carson; Wm Chambers; Thomas McBurney;

and William Carson

Thomas Allen, who made the deposition, viz.:

In January, 1842, Art O'Neill, in command of about eighty men, murdered John Millar in his house adjacent to the church, in which six men, three women and two boys had taken refuge.

William Kuming, senr. (called by his wife Cumings) was challenged to open the door on promise from O'Neill that he would not be molested. On gaining admittance O'Neill and his followers pinioned Charles Kuming, William Kuming, John Carson, Thomas McBurney, and William Maxwell, took them about a mile and a half away and murdered them.

Cf. *The Bloody Bridge*, p.98; Fitzpatrick

County Fermanagh

Creighton, Abraham – Drumboorey, Kinawley	July 9, 1617
Creighton, James – Aughalane, Lisnaskea	July 9, 1617
Creighton, Thomas – Aughalane	July 9, 1617
Cunningham, Gabriel	Feb. 12, 1619
Dunbar, Alexander	Feb. 12, 1619
Dunbar, George	Feb. 12, 1619
Dunbar, John	Feb. 12, 1619
Dunbar, James (his son)	Feb. 12, 1619
Erving, Christopher – Lettermoney	July 9, 1617
Gibb, James – Drumra	Aug. 29, 1610
Gibson, Robert – Aughnahinchmore	July 9, 1617
Hall, Robert-Royfad, parish of Boho	July 9, 1617
Hamilton, Malcom – Castletown	Aug. 17, 1617
Hamilton, James – Drumraye	Aug. 17, 1616
Hamilton, Robert, Derrynafogher	Aug. 29, 1616
Hamilton, Hugh, merchant – Loughneneas	July 9, 1617
Hamilton, Hugh – Moyah (Gent)	July 9, 1617
Heigate, James – Clankelly	Aug. 26, 1629
Johnson, James – Drumadown	July 9, 1617
Lindsay, Jerome	Feb. 12, 1619
Mitchell, Hugh – Reyfad, par. of Boho	July 9, 1617
Montgomery, Robert – Aughinlogher	Aug. 17, 1616

Patterson, Alexander –	Aug. 17, 1616
Smellham, George – Dirriany	Feb. 12, 1619
Somervell, Jamis – 'Tillikether'	Aug. 17, 1616
Stewart, Ludovic – Lurgabowy	Aug. 17, 1616

Tenants of Malcolm Hamilton
Chancellor of Down, afterwards Archbishop of Cashel
Freeholders:–
Robert Weir, Gabriel Cunningham and James Cunningham
Leaseholders:–

David Cathcart	Daniel Elliott
Alexander Cunningham	John Greer
David Cinningham, Junr	John Hall
Matthew Chambers	William Hall
Thomas Cranston	Gilbert Lainge
William Crawford	John Watson
George Deinbone	

Cf. *Inquisition Term* – (24) Chas. I
County Londonderry

Anderson, Robert	Aug. 17, 1617
Cawder, William	July 9, 1617
Cahoon, Andrew – Droghedonan	Nov. 1617
Cahoon, Peder – Droghedonan	Nov. 1617
Cunningham, James	July 9, 1617
Cunningham, William	July 9, 1617
Crawford, William – Droughedonan	Nov. 1617
Dykes, Andrew – Londonderry	May 28, 1617
English, Ninian, merchant – Londonderry	July 9, 1617
Gray, George, seaman	July 9, 1616
Johnston, Archibald	July 9, 1616
Keeland, John – Londonderry	July 9, 1616
Kennedy, Thomas – Coleraine	Nov. 1617
Kyle, James	July 9, 1616
Lindsay, Robert-seaman	July 9, 1616
Logy, James	July 9, 1616
Lynne, William – Derry City	July 9, 1616
Lyon, Andrew – Londonderry	Aug. 17, 1616

Lyon, Andrew – Londonderry	Aug. 17, 1617
McAlexander, Thomas, gent	July 9, 1616
McLornan, William-Moynevonen	Nov. 25, 1625
McNeile, Gilbert	July 9, 1617
Moncrieg, David	July 9, 1617
Moore John; seaman	July 9, 1617
Morton, Constantine	July 9, 1617
Patterson, John	July 9, 1617
Palmer, John; merchant – Londonderry	Aug. 17, 1617
Powr, John	Aug. 17, 1616
Redgate, Thomas; merchant – Londonderry	July 9, 1617
Russell, Robert-Londonderry (They were from Irvine)	Aug. 17, 1617
Sempell, Robert; clerk – Donaghheady	July 19, 1631
Thomas, Hugh; merchant – Londonderry	July 9, 1617
Thomson, Robert; merchant – Londonderry	July 9, 1617
Young, Rovert-Culdrum, Aghadowey	Nov. 28, 1625

Scots Settlers from other sources:
Buchanan, John – Coleraine, 1618
Andrews, John – 1622
Mure, William – Coleraine, 1618 (*Arch. Coll. of Ayr and Galloway, IX* p.30)

Sir Robert McLelland's Tenants

Sir Robert McLelland, of Bombee, in Scotland, Knt; freeholder of all those three townlands called Ballycashan, Lisronan, and Corboylan. [The townlands are minutely described]

Sir William Maxwell, of Gribbon in Scotland, Knt; freeholder to all that townland, called Ballereskmore

Herbert Maxwell, of Kurkennell in Scotland, gent; freeholder to half that townland called Enish Conoher.

Edward Fforester, of Culdoche in Scotland; gent; freeholder to all of that townland called Drumneere.

William Mackclellane, of Overlawe in Scotland; gent; freeholder to all that townland called Balle Monnevonne.

The names of the Six Freeholders in the nature of Copyholders:
John Edward, of Kircodboyth in Scotland; gent; freeholder to all that
townland called Crott

William Macklelland, of Molock in Scotland; gent; freeholder to half
that Townland called Drumleefe

William Magghee, of Kircubryt in Scotland; gent; freeholder to half
that Townland called Drumleefe

William Fullerton, of Kircubryt in Scotland; gent; freeholder to all
that Townland called Neekede

John Macklelland, of Bocbe [? Borgue] in Scotland; yeoman;
freeholder to half the Townland called Mean

John Macklelland, of Ochard in Scotland; yeoman; freeholder to half
that Townland called Macen.

Cf from a MS preserved in H.M. General Register House, Edinburgh,
and published in the Annual Report of the Pres. Hist. Soc., Belfast in
1909.

All the townlands named are in the County of Londonderry, in the
valley of the Roe.

Omitted: Alexander Mikell of Kircubryt in Scotland, Esq, freeholder,
to all that townland called Lislane

Monaghan
was not a Plantation County, and the Scots who settled in it were of
a more recent date.
    In the Muster of 1631 only 92 men were enrolled and none of them
appear to have been Scotch

County Tyrone

Abercorn, widow of Earl of Abercorn	May 12, 1620
Acheson, Janet; alias Lindsay – Tullyhoge	Feb. 12, 1619
Andrews, James – Strabane	Nov. 28, 1617
Arnett, Widow	Aug. 17, 1617
Arnett, Andrew – Strabane	Aug. 17, 1617
Boyle, John – Moyle Glebe, Ardstraw	Aug. 17, 1617
Boyle, William – Moyle Glebe, Ardstraw	Aug. 17, 1617

Brown, John	July 9, 1617
Burne, James	July 9, 1617
Carmichael, William – Island McHugh	Aug. 17, 1617
Carslaw, Matthew – Strabane	Aug. 17, 1617
Cathcart, Robert-Ballymanoch, Cookstown	May 20, 1617
Colville, Archibald; gent	July 9, 1617
Cooper, James – Strabane	Aug. 17, 1617
Craig, Alexander – Strabane	Aug. 17, 1617
Crawford, Matt.; servant to the Earl of Abercorn	July 9, 1617
Doninge, John – rufus, Donalong?	Aug. 17, 1617
Fingleton, John –	Feb. 12, 1619
Gamble, William – Ballymagarry, Leckpatrick	Feb. 12, 1619
Creire, Andrew – Findemoyne, Clogher; weaver	July 9, 1617
Drummond, Malcom –	May 29, 1629
(Cf. Hills *Plantation* p.534)	
Elpinstone, James	May 19, 1615
Gibbe, James – Strabane	July 9, 1617
Granger, Robert – Dunalong	Aug. 17, 1617
Ferry, James – Clary	Nov. 28, 1617
Hamilton, Archibald – Moyenner	March 24, 1629
Hamilton, Sir Claude	Feb. 12, 1620
Hamilton, Rev. Claudius	Aug. 17, 1617
Hamilton, Marion – 'Lisdivin'	July 19, 1631
Hamilton, Calude –Clericus; Clogher	Aug. 17, 1617
Hamilton, Hugh – gent; Movagh	July 9, 1617
Hamilton, James – merchant; Strabane	Aug. 27, 1617
Hamilton, James – servant to Earl of Abercorn	July 9, 1617
Hamilton, John – son of Patrick	July 9, 1617
Hamilton, Patrick – Clericus – Co Down	July 9, 1617
Hamilton, Robert; U.D.	July 9, 1617
Hamilton, Robert – Corrig	July 9, 1617
Hamilton, William – merchant; Strabane	July 9, 1617
Hamilton, Com. – Ballyfattan	July 9, 1617
Hatrick, James – Strabane	July 9, 1616
Henderson, John – tailor; Strabane	Aug. 17, 1616
Hexburn, Sir Robert –'Icanagan'	July 12, 1610
Highgate, James – Gortgammon	May 20, 1617

Highgate, James (and again)	Aug. 26, 1629
Kennedy, William – carpenter; Strabane	Aug. 17, 1616
Kyle, William – Strabane	Aug. 17, 1616
Love, William	July 9, 1616
Lawson, Peter – tailor; Strabane	Aug. 17, 1616
Lindsay, James – Magavelin	July 9, 1616
Lindsay, Robert – Tullyhoge	Jan 1, 1630
Lindsay, Janet – wife of above	Feb. 12, 1619
Lynn, David – Dunalong?	Aug. 17, 1616
Lynn, John – Dunalong?	Aug. 17, 1616
McCreaghan, Gilbert – Ballymagorry, Leckpatrick	Aug. 17, 1616
McCeaghan, Patrick – Ballymagorry, Leckpatrick	Aug. 17, 1616
McGraghan, Archd. – Ballymagorry, Leckpatrick	Aug. 17, 1616
McIntyre, John – Strabane	Aug. 17, 1617
Mackeson, George, M.A. (Dean of Armagh, which see)	Oct. 29, 1623
Montgomery, John – Ballymagorry	Nov. 28, 1617
Millar, Robert – Dunalong, Co Tyrone	Aug. 17, 1617
Montgomery, James – Tullonafert	July 9, 1617
Montgomery, Gilbert – Tullonafert	July 9, 1617
Morrison, David – Strabane	Aug. 17, 1617
Patterson, William – Strabane	Aug. 17, 1617
Pooke, James – Strabane	Aug. 17, 1617
Pringle, William – Callinganie	Nov. 28, 1630
Richardson, Alexander – Balliarskie	Dec. 16, 1630
Richardson, Alexander – Creige	Dec. 16, 1630
Saunderson, Alex. – Tullylagan, Cookstown	Sept. 26, 1614
Sharpe, James – Strabane	July 9, 1617
Simpson, Gabriel – Dunalong	Aug. 17, 1617
Spottiswood, Beatrix, alias Areskine	Oct. 29, 1623
Spottiswood, James; Bishop of Clogher	April 14, 1621
Spottiswood, Agnes (his wife)	Oct. 29, 1622
Spottiswood, Henry	Oct. 29, 1622
Stephenson, David – Strabane?	Aug. 17, 1617
Stephenson, John, senr – Strabane	Aug. 17, 1617
Stephenson, John, junr. – Strabane	July 9, 1617
Stephenson, John – Paknsbancke [Peacockbank]	July 9, 1617
Stephenson, Thomas	July 9, 1617

Stewart, Sir Andrew – Donaghenry	Feb. 26, 1629
Stewart, Henry – O'Caragan, Dungannon	March 3, 1629
Stewart, John – Ballyneagh, Cookstown	May 9, 1619
Stewart, Robert – Ballyrokevan	
Stewart, Patrick – Tieranonuriertagh	Feb. 12, 1619
Stewart, William	May 7, 1619
Symington, John – 'Gorteville'	Dec. 16, 1630
Wallace, John, senr. – Strabane	Aug. 17, 1629
Wooley, Robert – Strabane	Nov. 1617
Yoing, James – Clericus; Urney	July 9, 1617
Young, Thomas – Strabane	Aug. 17, 1617
Hamilton, Hugh – Loughneas, Leckpatrick	July 9, 1617

From other sources:
Kennedy, Fergus – Gortivelly 1618
Stewart, James, Patrick, Katherine – (Clapham), Ardschagh

Sir William Stewart's Tenants
On his lands in the neighbourhood of Clogher and Augher, purchased of Edward Kingsmill, May 10, 1616
Herbert Maxwell, on June 1st, 1616 for a term of 21 years, the Ballyboes called Mullaghvany, Proluske, and two-thirds of the Townland of Killany
David Barkley, Esq, – On Nov, 1st. 1620; for a term of 19 years, three Ballyboes.
Robert Murdogh; on May 1st, 1620; for a term of 5 years; one Ballyboe.
Between the years 1617 and 1627, Sir William set lands to the following tenants, for terms from 7 to 19 years.

Jane Demstar	David McKearne	John Montgomery
John Karns	John McIlmurry	William Morne
Andrew McCrery	Alex. McKittrick	Wm Morrow
Michl McCullough	Alex. Maxwell	Robt Murduff
Mule McGern	Wm Means	Roger Mean
John Meen	Philamy O'Neele	John Wilson
John Wright		

Cf. *Ul. Inquisition* – (49) Chas I

Sir John Drummond's Tenants:
On June 1st, 1622, he let his lands to the following tenants, most of whom were 'neer Irish'.

Beana, Thos.	McGunshenour, Neal	O'Sloddan, Neal
Crosby, John	McKaundy, Owen	O'Sloddan, Shane
Crosby, Com.	Muntreeth, Wm	Reade, Wm
Drum, Patrick	O'Donnelly, Gilduff	Sharp, William
Grime, John	O'Kearnon, Shane Duff	
Gryme, Thomas	O'Neale, Rory	Smyth, Patrick
McAulay, John	O'Quinn, Comogher	Wood, John
McGowan, John	O'Quinn, Hugh	O'Sloddan, Owen

Cf. Inquisition at Newtownstewart, Jan. 9. 1625
'Clogher na Righ', J.J. Marshall, M.A. p.77
William Pringle, from Torwoodlea, Scotland, settled at Coolnageerie, Ballygawley, in 1616, and was there in 1619 (Pynnar) Clogher, Co Tyrone

In 'Clogher na Righ', 1930, Mr J J Marshall, M.A., writes, (p.47) 'There is printed in the Calendar of State Papers, Ireland, 1611-14 (p.308) an order from the Lord Deputy to the Attorney General' to draw forth a fiant of incorporation to the Bishop of Clogher, Robert Montgomery, Provost:-

Gibson, Robert	Montgomery, John
Hamilton, James	Steward, David
Hendrie, Andrew	Steward, George
Montgomery, Gilbert	Steward, Ludovic
Montgomery Hugh	Wilie, John
Montgomery, James	

by the name of Provost and Burgesses of the town of Clogher, enabling them to send Burgesses to Parliament, and to enjoy other privileges, &c., according to the King's letters of Oath, December, 1612.

The above-named Provost and Burgesses were probably all Scots.

Strabane

An Inquisition taken at Strabane on 16 August, 1693, mentions the following tenants of the Baronscourt estate as having holdings in the **Town of Strabane:–**

Anderson, John	Love, John
McGee, James	
Hamilton, James	Lawes, Samuel
Newburgh, Ann	
Hamilton, Patrick	McCausland, Oliver
Parke, Andrew	
Henderson, William	McFarland, Walter
Robinson, Robert	
Holmes, Thomas	

Cf. Hills *Plantation* p.52 of 8
Cf Inquisition of Ulster; Gul. of Mary

The following were naturalised on 22 June, 1615, but their location is unknown

Blair, Alexander	Harvie, John
Blair, James	Millar, John
Boyle, Thos., senr	Moore, John
Futhy, Robert	Paton, William
Honis, Andrew	Russell, James
Hudgsone, George	Skingeor, Alexander
Hamilton, James	
Gamble, William	Aug. 17, 1616
Graham, Thomas	Feb. 12, 1619
Johnson, Archibald	July 9, 1616
Kyle, James	July 9, 1616
Lindsay, Robert	July 9, 1616
Haldane, Archibald?	Aug. 18, 1607
Logy, John	July 9, 1616
Trench, James; minister	Feb. 12, 1619
Barber, John; minister	Feb. 12, 1619

The Black Oath
While the National Convenant was being extensively signed in Scotland, and hostilities between the King and the Covenanters were daily becoming more apparent, Wentworth, the Lord Deputy, dreading

that the Scots in Ulster would take up arms and create a diversion in favour of their compatriots, informed the King that he had ready an army of four thousand men so strategically placed that they could pounce on them at the earliest indication of insurrection.

At the same time he intimated to his Majesty that he had received a petition, numerously signed by Scottish gentlemen, pointing out that the King might account them as conspirators, or, at least, in sympathy with the Covenanters. To put their loyalty beyond doubt they desired that an oath should be given them renouncing the National Covenant and asserting their complete submission to his Majesty's commands.

The Bishop of Raphoe drew up the petition which when corrected and approved by Wentworth, was signed by the following:–

Hugh Montgomery, 2nd Viscount, Ards
James Hamilton, Claneboy
James Spotiswood, Bishop of Clogher
John Leslie, Bishop of Raphoe
Henry Leslie, Bishop of Down and Connor
Andrew Stewart, 2nd Lord Castlestewart
Sir William Semple, Letterkenny
Sir Francis Hamilton, Killeshandra
Robert Hannay
Sir James Craig, Crighan Castle
Sir John Cunningham, Manorcunningham
Sir Robert Stewart, Culmore Fort
Sir Henry Dunbar, Co Fermanagh
Sir Thomas Bruce, Rector of Taboynee
Archibald Erskine, son-in-law to the Bishop of Cloger
William Maxwell, Bailieborough
Robert Maxwell, Dean of Armagh
John Echlin, son of the late Bishop of Down
Robert Bailie, Bailieborough
William Fullerton, Archdeacon of Armagh
William Hamilton, brother to Lord Claneboy
John Hamilton, brother to Lord Claneboy
William Richardson, Barony of Dungannon

Alexander Caldwell, Leaseholder
Archibald Hamilton, brother of Lord Claneboy
Captain James Wishart
Christopher Irwin, Co Fermanagh
Archibald Stewart, Ballinboy
Arthur Moneypenny, Prebedary of St Andrews (Kilarasey, Co Down)
Paul Reynolds, M.P. for Killyleagh
John Cunningham, son of Sir James Cunningham
Major James Galbraith
William Stewart, Laird of Dunduff
James Edmeston, Randox
Robert Leslie, Prebendary of Rasharkin, and son of Henry Leslie, Bishop of Down

Sir Francis Hamilton of Manorhamilton, and Sir James Montgomery of Greyabbey, refused to sign the petition.

The Oath was to be taken by every adult Scot, male and female, and was as follows:–

'I.....do faithfully swear, profess and promise that I will honour and obey my sovereign Lord, King Charles, and will bear faith and true allegiance to him, and will defend and maintain his regal power and authority, and that I will not bear arms or do any rebellious or hostile act against him or protest against any of his royal commands, but submit myself in all due obedience thereunto. And I will not enter into any covenant, oath or bond of mutual defence or assistance against any persons whatsoever, by force, without his Majesty's sovereign and regal authority.'

'And I denounce and abjure all covenants, oaths and bonds whatsoever, contrary to that I have herein sworn, professed, and promised, so help me God in Christ Jesus.'

Carved in Stone: A Record of Memorials in the Ancient Graveyard around the Church of the Holy Evangelists at Carnmoney, by the Belfast Branch, North of Ireland Family History Society, 1994, 138pp, ISBN 0-9524698-0-4, £7-50

The graveyard of Carnmoney Parish Church on the northern outskirts of Belfast is one of the most interesting in Ulster because of its antiquity and size and of the number of eminent citizens buried therein. Project Leader William Stewart and his team of enthusiasts from the Belfast Branch of the North of Ireland Family History Society are therefore to be congratulated on the completion of the immense task of accessing, cleaning up, and recording the inscriptions on the graveyard's 721 memorials, many of which were submerged in undergrowth when the project began in the Autumn of 1993.

In the resultant publication, with its photographs of ten of the most notable stones and an equal number of illustrations beautifully drawn by Caryl Sibbett, the inscriptions are detailed in alphabetical order of surnames, and all surnames mentioned on stones are indexed. New maps specially prepared for the publication show the locations of the 852 numbered plots in the graveyard; and the appropriate plot number is quoted in each recorded inscription, permitting rapid pinpointing of any particular grave.

The publication shows other user-friendly innovations. For example, there is an index to placenames that appear in the inscriptions, with cross-referencing to surnames and plot numbers. Likewise, there is a separate surname/plot-number index for each of the graveyard's seven sections, together with a list of the memorials inside the church. To the very limited extent that occupations of the deceased are recorded on the gravestones, these too have been indexed. However, in contrast to the current practice of the Ulster Historical Foundation in its *Gravestone Inscriptions* series, no attempt has been made to set the inscriptions in context by adding externally-researched biographical details and/or information derived from registries of wills.

In an introductory article on the history of the parish (known in earlier times as Coole) David Honneyman, Past President of the North of Ireland Family History Society, makes brief reference to seven notable families who buried in the churchyard. His list includes the Biggars, the Grimshaws, and the Leppers, families that have long been of interest to students of the industrial, commercial, and political heritage of Ulster; and I was able to fill many gaps in my own records of these families by reference to the relevant gravestone inscriptions recorded in this volume. But that in turn led me to peruse the publication more systematically, in search of records of additional families or individuals who had contributed notably to the commercial, professional, or political life of the province over the past 200 years – and I was not disappointed, for I found many that met that specification.

One such family was the McCalmonts of Abbeylands, buried in plots E120 and E121. In the late eighteenth and early nineteenth century the then head of the dynasty, Hugh McCalmont (*ca* 1766-1838), made a sufficient impact on the business life of Belfast to be appointed to the first Board of Superintendence of the Belfast Banking Company in 1827.[1] In a later generation another Hugh (born *ca* 1810) made a fortune as a stockbroker in London and was worth around £3 million when he died at Abbeylands in 1887.[2] The family also provided distinguished military men and several MPs for Antrim constituencies, one of whom is buried in Carnmoney: that is James Martin McCalmont (1847-1913). Of the soldiering McCalmonts the most notable to be buried there is Brigadier-General Sir Robert C A McCalmont, KCVO CBE DSO, Irish Guards, who was born in 1881 and died in 1953. In total, the two McCalmont stones in Carnmoney provide records of the lifespans of 12 members of that distinguished family.

The occupants of another famous house in the Whiteabbey area were buried in plot number GO31: these were the Valentines of Glenavna, which is now the site of the hotel of that name. The most notable member of that family was William Valentine (*ca* 1813-1894) who after a career in the linen industry became President of the Belfast Chamber of Commerce (1853/54); the owner for a time of Fortwilliam Park and builder of its ornamental entrances;[3] and a director (1857-1877) and later Chairman (1877-1894) of the Northern Banking Company Ltd.[4]

A broken and worn stone on plot number D151 marks the grave of

Edmund Getty (1799-1857), Ballast Master of the old Belfast Harbour Corporation from 1837 till 1847 and the first Secretary of the Belfast Harbour Commissioners, from 1847 till 1857.[5] Edmund Getty was the son of Robert Getty, foundation member of the Belfast Chamber of Commerce and prominent activist in the radical movement at the end of the 18th century.[6] The younger Getty's mother was a daughter of Nicholas Grimshaw of Whitehouse (*vide infra*).[7]

Some 50 members of the Grimshaw family are buried in seven plots in the graveyard (numbers D088, D089, D090, E140, E141, E142, and G174); and Robert Grimshaw JP DL of Longwood, who died in 1867 aged 80, is additionally remembered by stained glass windows in the parish church. The member of the family who arguably made the greatest impact on the industrial and commercial life of Ulster was Nicholas (1748-1805), son of another Nicholas (*ca* 1714-1777) and of Susannah (*nee* Briarcliffe): he came to Belfast from Lancashire in 1776; set up a textile printing business at Greencastle; advised on the experimental establishment of cotton manufacture in the Belfast Charitable Society's Poorhouse in 1778; and established a large cotton mill at Whitehouse in the 1780s, initially in partnership with Nathaniel Wilson.[8] He has therefore often been described as 'the father of cotton manufacture in this country'.

In the next generation Nicholas Grimshaw's various enterprises were carried on by his sons including Edmund (*ca* 1777-1854) who lived at Mossley and converted the printworks there into a flax-spinning mill,[9] and the very versatile Robert (*vide supra*) who inherited the family seat at Longwood. Unlike his father, Robert did not devote his time exclusively to his own industrial activities but was active as well in many outside bodies including the boards of two of Ulster's early railway companies; the successive organisations that controlled the Port of Belfast; the Belfast Chamber of Commerce, where he was a council member for almost 30 years, becoming President in 1857/58; and, above all, the Ulster Bank, which he helped to establish in 1836 and which he served as a director from then till the day of his death at the age of 80 – death brought about, poignantly, by a fall on a flight of steps in the bank's head office building in Waring Street.[10,11]

Another old Belfast cotton and banking family, the Leppers of Trainfield House and Elsinore (Crawfordsburn), occupy no less than

11 plots in the graveyard (A60-63, C68/69, and G176-180). The first head of the family, Francis Lepper of late eighteenth and early nineteenth century fame, is not buried in Carnmoney, but is mentioned on two gravestones there as the father of Robert Stewart Lepper (1812-1866) and of Charles William Lepper (1824-1883). In partnership with John McCrum (who may also have stemmed from a Carnmoney family), Francis Lepper opened a huge cotton mill on the Antrim Road in Belfast in 1811.[12] Burned to the ground in February 1813, the mill was re-built within a year[13] and seems to have remained in the control of the Lepper family for the next 50 years or thereabouts. The family also produced a senior director of the Ulster Bank, Francis Robert Lepper (*ca* 1846-1908), a grandson of the original Francis Lepper – and he is buried in Carnmoney.

Perhaps the most colourful public figure to be buried there is Joseph Gillis Bigger (1828-1890). His grave is to be found in plot number G052, one of eight plots where the gravestones bear references to members of the Bigger or Biggar families. Joe Bigger, as he became known, was a Belfast pork butcher who at the age of 40 entered the political arena via Belfast Town Council before becoming Nationalist MP for County Cavan. Despite his staunch Presbyterian background, Bigger had by then become an ardent Home Ruler; and, after a relatively short flirtation with the Irish Republican Brotherhood, he joined the Roman Catholic Church and continued in that communion till the end of his life. It was of Joe Bigger that an observer of the Westminster scene once wrote: 'When the member for Cavan rises to address the House, a whiff of salt pork seems to float upon the gale!'. This colourful and enigmatic character featured prominently in an interesting article on Carnmoney Cemetery by Dr Eamon Phoenix, published in the *Ulster Tatler* in 1984.[14]

The Rt Hon William K Fitzsimmons, a politician of a different hue and a different era, is remembered on a gravestone in plot number D140: he died in 1992. The shipbuilding industry is represented by Alexander Connell (*ca* 1808-1875) who in 1844 succeeded his father in Charles Connell & Sons' yard on the Antrim side of Belfast Lough. The Samuel Gelston of Rosstulla, buried in plot number G082, is likely to have been the person who joined John Dunville in his whiskey business in 1825 after the death of his first partner, William Napier.[15]

Aaron Staunton (*ca* 1787-1877) buried in plot number D028 had two sons, Moses and Aaron, who started Carnmoney Cotton Printing Works in partnership with David Bigger. And Gordon Augustus Thomson (1799-1886), the last of the famous Thomsons of Jennymount, is remembered on a stone in plot number F080.

These are but snippets of the stories that lie behind some the records now preserved in *Carved in Stone*; and there can be no doubt that the inclusion of information of this nature would have added substantially to the interest of the publication to general readers. But for the professional genealogist or the enthusiastic amateur in pursuit of his or her roots in the Carnmoney area the publication in its present form is a most useful addition to the range of sources available; and the Belfast Branch of the North of Ireland Family History Society is again to be complimented on bringing this great project to fruition.

George Chambers

NOTES

1. S Shannon Millin, *Additional Sidelights on Belfast History*, W & G Baird, Belfast, 1938, p 154.
2. Kate Newman, *Dictionary of Ulster Biography*, Institute of Irish Studies QUB, 1993, p 147.
3. J Flanaghan, *Belfast Telegraph*, 13 April 1985.
4. E D Hill, *The Centenary Volume of the Northern Banking Company Ltd Belfast*, McCaw, Stevenson, and Orr, Belfast, 1925, pp 92/93.
5. D J Owen, *A Short History of the Port of Belfast*, Mayne, Boyd, and Son, 1917, p 385.
6. George Chambers, *Familia*, Vol 2, No 10, Ulster Historical Foundation, 1994, pp 13-38.
7. George Benn, *A History of the Town of Belfast from 1799 till 1810*, Marcus Ward, 1880, p 225.
8. George Chambers, *Faces of Change*, NI Chamber of Commerce & Industry, Belfast, 1983, p 105.
9. Angelique Day & Patrick McWilliams (Eds), *Ordnance Survey Memoirs of Ireland, Vol Two, Parishes of Co Antrim (i) 1838-9*, Institute of Irish Studies, Belfast, 1990, pp 47/48.
10. C E B Brett, *Buildings of Belfast 1700-1914*, Revised Edition, Friar's Bush Press, 1985, pp 38, 44.
11. George Platt, archivist Ulster Bank, personal communication.
12. J C Beckett & R E Glasscock (Eds), *Belfast: the Origin and Growth of an Industrial City*, British Broadcasting Corporation, 1967, p 83.
13. Jonathan Bardon, *Belfast: An Illustrated History*, Blackstaff Press, Belfast, 1982, p 67).
14. Eamon Phoenix, *Ulster Tatler*, November 1984, pp 81/83.
15. S Shannon Millin, *Sidelights on Belfast History*, W & G Baird, Belfast, 1932, p 72.

An Index to the Newtownards Chronicle 1901-1939, compiled by Kenneth Robinson, published by the Library & Information Service, South Eastern Education & Library Board, 1995. ISBN 0-9509047-7-5. £5-00.

It was in 1983 that the South Eastern Education & Library Board published the first of its series of indexes of County Down newspapers: that volume dealt with the *County Down Spectator 1904-1964* and was compiled by the late Jack McCoy, a dedicated member of staff in the Irish Section at the Board's Library Headquarters in Ballynahinch. Further volumes from the same compiler followed in 1984 and 1987: these related respectively to the *Mourne Observer 1949-1980* and the *Down Recorder 1836-1886*. Next to appear was a volume dealing primarily with the *Newtownards Chronicle 1873-1900*, but also with the four-year run of the *Newtownards Independent 1871-1873*: this was compiled by Kenneth Robinson and published by the Board in 1990. Now this valuable quartet has become a quintet, with the addition of a volume dealing with the *Newtownards Chronicle 1901-1939*. Kenneth Robinson is again the very perceptive compiler; and the value of the volume is enhanced by a most interesting introduction from the pen of Dr Trevor McCavery, author of a recent history of Newtownards.

Like its predecessors this index to selected items in the successive issues of the newspaper over a period of 39 years is a mine of information for the local historian and the genealogist – and even for the less committed reader who wishes simply to be reminded of or to learn for the first time about life in County Down in earlier times, including glimpses of the impact in the county of provincial, national, and world events. The 5,815 entries are arranged chronologically; and they are each of sufficient length to be informative in themselves, as well as pointing to the availability of the complete articles and news items on microfilm within the Library Service of the South Eastern Board. And to facilitate rapid searching, the volume includes two 'indexes to the index', covering over 1,250 places and subjects, and some 1,400 named individuals.

Amongst the families that feature most frequently in the index are the Andrews of Comber, the Dufferins of Clandeboye, the Dunleaths

125

of Ballywalter, the Londonderrys of Mount Stewart, the Nugents of Portaferry, and the Sharman-Crawfords of Crawfordsburn. But there is room too for a baker from Bangor, a school teacher from Lisbane, a bank manager from Newtownards, a missionary from Ballywalter, a stationmaster from Donaghadee – and many hundreds of other ordinary people whose descendants around the world would find interest and inspiration in the information signposted in this volume. Likewise for the student of local history, there is an abundance of fascinating subjects within these pages – from the evangelical preaching of the Rev W. P. Nicholson in Bangor to illicit distilling at Ballynahinch; from 'ping pong' in Ballywalter to hare coursing in Donaghadee; from the institution of the Gaelic League in Portaferry to the opening of 'another Fort of loyalty' (an Orange hall) in Killinchy; and from the great Tourist Trophy road races on the Ards Circuit to Harry Ferguson's pioneering flights in various parts of the county.

This volume and its predecessors are rich sources for those interested in the history and genealogy of County Down, as are the parallel indexes to Down and Lisburn items in the *Northern Star 1792-1797* and the *Northern Herald 1833-1836*. These too were compiled by Jack McCoy and published by the South Eastern Board. All seven publications are still in print and can be obtained singly or in combinations from the Irish & Local Studies Section, South Eastern Education & Library Board, Windmill Hill, Ballynahinch, Co Down BT24 8DH; or from the Ulster Historical Foundation's *Familia* bookshop at 64 Wellington Place, Belfast BT1 6GE.

George Chambers

Oceans of Consolation: Personal Accounts of Irish Migration to Australia by David Fitzpatrick. Cork University Press 1995. £37.50 Hardcover, £19.50 Paperback.

This book surely breaks new ground in the study of the emigrant experience. It is particularly fitting that its year of publication coincides with the beginning of the commemorative events of the Great Famine years because the popular mind invariably associates the Irish diaspora with the the effects of the Famine. Yet readers who suppose this work to be a mere compilation of migrant Irish-Australian letters will find their assumptions to be sadly wanting. Fitzpatrick explores fourteen sequences of emigrant letters, eleven of them sent from Australia to Ireland and three sent the other way, between the 1830s and the 1880s. The book is produced consciously on two levels: the more commonplace level of reproducing edited extracts from each set of family letters with a commentary on the wider backgrounds of the families concerned, and the representations they contain both of the worlds of the writers and the writers' perceptions of the worlds of the recipients.

All features of the emigrant story are here, or at least many of them, portrayed through family chronicles. They illustrate some of the basic themes in Irish emigration historiography: the types of people who chose to emigrate, in the broadest demographic sense, for emigration was, as Fitzpatrick underscores, analogous to marriage in its significance in most Irish lives; the likely determinants of the decision to go; the organisation involved, the chain of movements; and the fluidity of the work experience as emigrants became settlers. Other aspects engage a fresh angle such as the letters from the Daltons in mid nineteenth-century Tipperary which evoke the contemporary acceptance of the emptying of the Irish countryside – 'I road by your little Cottage a few days ago and the thisels were growing in the middle of the road' (p. 546). Fitzpatrick's selection also stresses that the Irish-Australian movement was far from an aberrant offshoot but an integral element of a world-wide dispersion. As such, he proposes no radical differences between the 'stock' of Irish-Australians and Irish-Americans. For this reader the three collections of letters from families with Ulster connections are particularly interesting for their insights on conditions back home in Ireland. The Hammonds from County Armagh and the Brennans from County Down whose homes in Ireland were only about fifteen miles apart, and the Fifes from County Fermanagh, all reveal in their correspondence their connections with the linen industry, in growing flax for sale, as workers in domestic weaving and warping and in sewing whitework. For none of the families was linen their chief support and they eked out an unstable subsistence by combining it with farming. William Fife expressed scepticism about investing in flax growing in the early 1860s, writing to an emigrant offspring that 'there has not been as much flax sowed in Ireland for the last twenty years ... It will do a Great Deal of Good or a deal of harm' (p. 419). The toil of families engaged in domestic weaving, even of fine diapers, is described in an 1864 letter to Helena Hammond in Victoria from her sister Susanna in Bleary, County Armagh. Susanna's four grown-up daughters wove at home on hand looms and were joined in their labour by their three younger sisters when they came home from school. At the level of representation of the emigrants' world, the letters from Australia provide evidence as to the selection of information which the writers thought their readers should know. Thus the emphases on educating the children and also on states of health or illness are viewed in part as responses to explicit and implicit appeals for financial help from their Irish connections. The letters home also contain depictions of novelty at all levels of everyday living in an empty land, from the vastness of the distances, the bewildering differences in farming because of the climate and soil, the wages and jobs, the descriptions of housing materials and the profusion of provisions,

The use of these letters as life documents is greatly extended by the family photographs from both sides of the ocean, a testimony to the care of the author in seeking out a reconstruction of the past. To these are added more publicly-accessible images, requiring no less thoroughness in research, from contemporary magazines and archive collections. The totality of this innovative interpretation sets new standards for future research methods in a wide range of historical themes.

Brenda Collins

Flax to Fabric: The Story of Irish Linen, by Brenda Collins. An Irish Linen Centre and Lisburn Museum publication. 1994. £4.50.

Flax to Fabric outlines the establishment, development and decline of what was, for some three centuries, Ireland's, particularly Ulster's, principal manufacturing industry. The story of linen is, consequently, central to an informed understanding of the fabric, in more senses than one, of the island's society and economy in modern times. The introductory chapter of this attractively-designed and illustrated publication outlines the importance of linen cloth and its manufacture in domestic industry of Biblical and mediaeval societies. It traces the linen industry's association with the north-eastern corner of Ireland and describes the role of linen not only in the pre-industrial economy but also in the development of landlord relations which characterised Ulster in the eighteenth and nineteenth centuries.

The myth that the linen industry was brought to Ireland by the Huguenots is firmly de-bunked, though their role in the development of the industry in the early eighteenth century is accorded due prominence. The critical changes in the manufacture of linen, including the introduction of machine-spun yarn from the 1830s, and the subsequent industrialisation of the industry, had critical implications for the Ulster farming community. The loss of a supplementary income from the home manufacture of linen helped dislodge the roots of many from the land, and prompted a migration to a town or city in Ulster, or to Britain, or across the Atlantic and often, successively, all three.

It was the industrialisation of the industry which saw Lisburn become a major provincial centre for linen, a role which is suitably described in the exhibitions on display in the Irish Linen Centre of the award-winning Lisburn museum, of which it is part. The volume under review relates closely to the historical material and reflects the quality of displays evident in both. It should lead the inquiring genealogist to a better understanding of the society from which their forebears emigrated and the social and economic circumstances which prompted their decision to leave, a consideration rarely articulated in other records.

Trevor Parkhill

9 780901 905734

www.ingramcontent.com/pod-product-compliance
Lightning Source LLC
Chambersburg PA
CBHW021833020426
42334CB00014B/601